IF IT WEREN'T FOR YOU, WE COULD GET ALONG!

Stop blaming & Start living

Other Books of Interest:

DC Press

Raising Children One Day at a Time:
A Daily Survival Guide
for Committed Parents

Who's Right (Whose Right?):
Seeking Answers and Dignity in the
Debate Over the Right to Die

E-R: From Prevention to Triage
— How to Retain Key Employees

How to Compete in the War for Talent:
A Guide to Hiring the Best

InSync Press

Go for the Green!
Leadership Secrets from the Golf Course (the Front Nine)

366 Surefire Ways to Let Your Employees Know
They Count

Retain or Retrain:
How to Keep the Good Ones from Leaving

IF IT WEREN'T FOR YOU, FOR YOU, WE COULD GET ALONG!

Stop blaming & Start living

Lewis E. Losoncy

PRESS

A Division of the Diogenes Consortium

SANFORD • FLORIDA

Published by DC Press
2445 River Tree Circle
Sanford, FL 32771
http://www.focusonethics.com
407-688-1156

This book was set in Trump Medieaval
Cover Design and Composition by Jonathan Pennell

Library of Congress Catalog Number: 2001000000
        Losoncy, Lewis E.
If It Weren't For You, We Could Get Along
        ISBN: 0-9708444-3-3

First DC Press Edition
10   9   8   7   6   5   4   3   2   1
Printed in the United States of America

DEDICATIONS

To Diane, Gabrielle & Tyler,

If it weren't for you...
I wouldn't fully understand love

To Albert Ellis,

If it weren't for you...
I'd still be thinking I'm an effect, not a cause

To Arnie & Sydell Miller,

If it weren't for you...

I wouldn't know that a few people can
change a whole industry

To Sen. Mike O'Pake, Dr. Gust Zogas,
Charlie Adams & Jack Holcomb,

If it weren't for you...

I wouldn't be aware that a whole community's
spirit could be lifted by a few people who

committed their life to legislating, educating,
creating, and elevating their constituents,
students, audience and listeners

To Dennis McClellan,

If it weren't for you...

I would not have put my heart into
this book.

To the Matrix Chain Gang,

All for one purpose

THANKS FROM A PRETZEL LOVER

ACKNOWLEDGMENTS

T O DENNIS McCLELLAN, publisher of DC Press, simply a genius who every author in the world needs to meet. You are an author's dream.

To Cindy and Marnee McClellan for their support and friendship.

To Lauren Losoncy, tennis pro, said ahead of time.

To Ron and Kim Losoncy, Aimee and Eric Oxenreider.

To my friends Len Marrella, Don Sanders, Ed Rose, Tom Chlebos and Dick Cahn.

To my teammates at Matrix Essentials, Bob Niles, Michael Pecce, Philip Clough, Bob Cassau, Mary Wilson, Judy McGlinn and Alan Stockman.

To Ron Beible and long time friend Paul Henry. And a special thanks to Ginny Guinn.

To Emily Dando, Lindsay Bell, Caroline Reese, Alex Bellows, Marjorie Berman, Colleen McNichol, Katie Ertel, Hannah Smith, Nicole Fiddler, Callie Eardley, Emily Vogel, Erika Dicky, Jennifer Kline, Jack Dando, Amelia DiPillo, Marissa DiPillo, Melanie Morris, Ashley Morris, Katie

Smith, P.J. Smith, Stacey & Mallory Seigfried, Madison Smith, Kirsten Pollins and Hallie Peterson.

To Craig Wolfel, Laura Gawthrop, Lauren Bollinger, Stephen Karst, Wendy Renier and our special friend, Andrea.

Thanks to all of you, for your inspiration. If it weren't for you...!

ABOUT THE AUTHOR

L EW LOSONCY IS A PSYCHOLOGIST and author of 17 books on the topics of encouragement, motivation, teamwork and positive attitude. Dr. Losoncy is the psychologist for Matrix Essentials, North America's largest producer of Professional Beauty Products. Matrix is a division of L'Oreal.

Other recent books by Losoncy include **Turning People On**, **Today: Grab it!**, **What is, is!** with Diane Losoncy, **The Motivating Team Leader**, **The Skills of Encouragement** & **The Best Team Skills**.

"Dr. Lew" has spoken in all 50 U.S. States, most of the Provinces of Canada, throughout Australia and New Zealand, as well as Mexico, France and England. He has appeared on TV programs such as *CNN* and *CBS This Morning*, and in media as varied as *The Wall Street Journal*, *Psychology Today*, and *Talk*.

PUBLISHER'S COMMENT

WITH 60,000 BOOKS being pumped out annually in this country, it is difficult to find those that can stand out from the crowd— those that can make you really think or provide you with real food for thought and supply tools for making significant changes in one's life. Lew Losoncy has created such a book.

The central theme behind the books that DC Press publishes is simple: we want to provide the reading public with ways of impacting their own lives (as well as those they come in contact with), making changes, influencing others —all within ethically acceptable ways. It is our sincere hope that our publications will offer encouragement to readers, while supplying an element of spirit, while building character, and making it clear that nothing is done without volition.

Dr. Losoncy has been speaking to and writing for hundreds of thousands of people across the United States and in many countries around the world for the past two decades. His focus has always been that one can improve his or her own lot in life by accepting that what is, is and that by taking responsibility for the things that one does and for the things that one can change, life can be generally better and more rewarding. It is his strong belief that even under the worst of conditions and when facing terrible situations, an individual can still be true to themselves and show strength of character and positive decision-making skills.

One need not be buried under the rubble that others create. Dr. Losoncy shows throughout this book that blame can be a terminal illness. Some just never survive. Others, on the other hand, seem to have the skills (similar to strong antibodies that fight disease) to overcome and surmount obstacles that can cause personal defeat and life long feelings of failure and inadequacy. Throughout the pages of *If It Weren't For You, We Could Get Along* readers will find one practical suggestion after another for taking control of what goes on around them and how to add significant longevity to their lives. The techniques aren't difficult; the results can only be positive. The toughest obstacle to face is YOU. Don't let anger, frustration, and blame consume you. Take control and learn the skills of letting go, stop the blame game, and move forward immediately.

Dennis McClellan
Publisher, DC Press

PREFACE

5 Years from Now, Which Decision Will You Wish... You Made Today?

Continue to...

1. blame that other person, or get over it?

2. blame your past, or build your future?

3. blame your weaknesses and fears, or use your strengths?

4. blame the outer world, or develop your inner confidence?

5. blame reality, or accept what is?

6. blame people at home or work, or encourage them?

7. blame that huge challenge in front of you, or conquer it?

Whatever your choice, 5 years from now will arrive, very soon...

> *Continuing to blame will find you right where you are today...*

> *Living will give you five more years of life. And then some.*

This book will develop your practical intelligence to stop blaming, and to start living

CONTENTS

INTRODUCTION

We Give Our Power Away to Whatever We Blame!

INTELLIGENCE & PRACTICAL INTELLIGENCE QUOTIENT (P.I.Q.)

Intelligence is the speed of one's ability to make accurate connections between cause and effect. One's practical intelligence quotient is one's ability to take effective actions, in everyday life experiences, based on those connections. Happiness and success are products of one's practical intelligence quotient.

In one conversation, you can easily spot a person with a high practical intelligence quotient. This person has found an approach to life that works for him or her. Almost immediately, you sense this person's demeanor is being guided by hope. You appreciate her openness to accept, and then plow through tough setbacks, experiencing only a few momentary bumps. The only remains left of the tough times are her important lessons learned, sprinkled with dashes of philosophical humor. You're moved by her upbeat attitude, and unbending determination to rise above the obstacles ahead in her path. You just know that she is going to make it, even against all odds.

She is quite intelligent, in a very practical way. Her approach to life is extremely effective. She has made accurate connections between her view of life, which is the cause, and the resultant quality of her life. And then she demonstrates practical intelligence by acting on her learnings.

When you think about it, you also sense something else in this person. She is wasting little or no time building a case to blame someone, or something else, for her life. This frees her up to focus her energies forward to design her destiny. No wonder she is an optimist. She is going places.

A person with highly developed practical intelligence is taking his or her life circumstances, and molding them with a workable mental attitude to move their life forward. This person is finding ways to live life, to actualize their possibilities, rather than accumulating ways to blame life.

Compare her to the person who hasn't developed his practical intelligence. He is continuously down and out. He is still "stuck" on either other people, (which he may refer to, as something similar to "rats") or other events (which they describe as horrible, awful, terrible) in his life. He even elevates these people, or events, to the level of being the "cause," the undisputed source, of what he is still helplessly going through today. Its almost as if he is saying under-

neath, "If only it weren't for this or that, I could be successful and happy!"

The strain on his troubled face reveals the pain of car-
rying this heavy baggage of blame with him. You are becoming a little less quick to agree to help him lift his weighty
worries. You tried that before when you agreed that he is
justified in his anger or pain. Yes, he was "done in!" And
perhaps you noticed that your agreement only added further
support to his immobility.

Of course, he has a right to feel pain, anger, persecution
or whatever he is feeling. The issue here is not is he justified
in his anger or hurt. The question here is, "is it wise? Does
blaming something or someone else help him? Will he
grow? Will he get over it, and bring on a new day? Not as
long as he is blaming.

You can help. How? By assisting him to develop his practical intelligence. By encouraging him to put his blame baggage down. And then to go forward. You can help him to
stop blaming, and to start living.

People who spend their time blaming, rather than creating a new life direct their thoughts, feelings and energy to
dwell on the useless. Practically, that isn't very productive.
Instead of learning from the experience, and moving forward
enriched, they consume their present life in unproductive
seething and hurt. You notice that the theme in their life is,
"If only it weren't for..........., then I could have...........!"

The theme has become such a part of their life that it
just never occurs to them that it was neither the event, nor

the person that "caused" them to be stuck, hurt or angry. Rather, the person who has developed their practical intelligence is aware that it was their belief that, "If it weren't for............!" that is causing their misery. They know that when we blame someone or something else for our unhappiness, we, at that moment, give our power away to that person or event. Then, we have to wait for these powerful forces that pull our string to change. That approach is neither empowering, wise or practical.

We only have two and one half billion seconds of life to live. How many of these seconds do we want to use up consumed in helplessness, or revenge to one other person, in this huge world of six billion people? At some transforming moment, we gain the life changing awareness that, "Even if no one in my life changes, and even if I had this horrible past, I can take charge of my life, right here in this powerful moment called now."

How do we develop our practical intelligence quotient, and bring our power back to you? How do we find our center? By stop blaming, and start living!

Listen for the "If it weren't for's.......!"

Take a few seconds and think about the people near you, at home or at work. What are the things or the people that they are blaming for making their life miserable?

- other people

- the past

- fears and weaknesses

- no confidence & lack of support from strong others

- reality

- the people at the workplace

- the huge challenge ahead

These may range from other people, or events in their past. Or they may even be blaming their own fears, lack of confidence, bad luck, limited education, pessimism for holding them back.

Listen carefully for the reasons why they can't be more, do more, sell more, and live more. Listen for their, "If it weren't for's....."

"If it weren't for _____ ,_____ ,_____ ,_____ , etc.,

I could be _____ !"

Does Blaming = Giving Power Away?

It is vital for you to stop for a moment, and think. As you think about their belief you may experience the awesome power they have given to these people and experiences they are blaming. These blame sources have power over them only because they have given them power in the form of blame.

What we blame, "If it weren't for...!" we give our power away because we are saying, "I absolutely can't be happy, successful, positive, etc., until YOU change." My well-being depends upon YOU! YOU control me! So I must wait, and wait, and wait. Blame, and blame, and blame.

BLAMING IS INACCURATE

In addition to giving power away by blaming, blaming is inaccurate. Seems that if something like blaming is both ineffective and inaccurate, than it isn't very wise to continue doing it.

How is blaming inaccurate? Look at those blame sentences you listed again. Did these blame sources automatically create their resultant attitude? If 1,000 people all experienced the same horrible setbacks from these rotten people and tragedies, would all 1,000 people be equally upset? Or would there be a range of reactions from total devastation on one side to self-determination, motivation and renewal on the other?

Is it possible that two different people experiencing the same event respond to the event in two different ways, resulting in two different outcomes?

Who will walk away more happy and successful?

The one who blames, "If it weren't for...!" or the one who creates, "Because of that experience, I learned that I am going to do this or that. Without that experience I would not have learned this same information."

Blaming not only gives away our power, but blaming is inaccurate because the event did not cause my attitude. I caused my attitude towards the event. Notice the accurate and effective connection between cause and effect: I caused my effects of bouncing back quickly from that difficult experience. I cause the effects that I get.

To me, the two most significant people of the past century who helped us realize our practical intelligence power were psychiatrist Alfred Adler, and psychologist Albert Ellis. Adler, in the early part of the century concluded that neither heredity, nor environment determine us. They are just the building blocks that we construct to design ourselves. When we blame, we act "as if," we live in a faulty building and we can't do anything about it until the builder comes back, apologizes and rebuilds us a mansion. Then we could be happy.

Albert Ellis is founder of Rational-Emotive-Behavioral Therapy (REBT), and Co-author of numerous books, including the life changing, *A New Guide to Rational Living*. Ellis, who is considered by the popular Psychology Today Magazine as one of the leading thinkers of the last century, argued that life is as simple as, A-B-C.

At A is an **A**ctivating event. Someone does something to us that activates us to think about the event.

At C is our **C**onsequent emotion.

Before Ellis, we thought A the **A**ctivating event caused C, our **C**onsequent emotion. But, as we stated before, events don't cause emotions because if many people all experience the same A, they would have different reactions at C.

What then caused C, or our Consequent emotion?

The answer is B or our **B**elief about A. And we are in control of determining our belief. We are in control of our life. If at B, we believe we should Blame A, we will be hurt, or angry at C. If, however, at B, we **B**egin to move on with what Ellis calls, Rational Thinking, then at C, or at our **C**onsequent emotion, we create different results.

WOULD I THEN BE HAPPY IF THESE THINGS I BLAME, DIDN'T HAPPEN TO ME?

Blaming also is inaccurate because it assumes that had these things not happened to the person, then, then they would be happy and successful. Think about a person's sources of blame ask yourself the question, "If these sources of blame were not there, would this person truly be then what they think they could have been? Would it have been guaranteed?"

Of course not!

EITHER YOU DETERMINE YOUR ATTITUDE, OR SOMEONE ELSE WILL!

You are the CEO of your world. You determine what you put into, and what you take away, from each day. You cast the only, and deciding vote, on how you act and react to the events and circumstances in Your World. As CEO of your world, you have three major resources, or attitude tools at your disposal. You direct these three attitude power tools, that is, (1) your thoughts, (2) your emotions, and (3) your actions to work for you, or against you.

In fact, either you determine your attitude, or someone else will!

Think about it this way:

You are one self. Within that oneself, physically speaking, you are your body. Within your one self, socially speaking, you are your relationships with others. Spiritually speaking you are your relationship with your God.

And psychologically speaking, you are your attitude.

Consequently, your attitude towards your own self, your life and other people has a dramatic effect upon your life. There is only one thing more powerful than your attitude.

WHAT CAN BE MORE IMPORTANT THAN YOUR ATTITUDE?

You are more powerful than your attitude. Why? You direct and determine your attitude.

You can remember very conscious moments in which you decided what your attitude was going to be towards another person, can't you? Perhaps you were angry at someone else, say someone younger than you. And then, in a moment of using your practical intelligence, you pause, re-routed your blaming direction and thought, something like,

"Well, she sure isn't perfect. And I'm not perfect either. Let me give her a break. She's just a kid!"

Your conscious, controlling, directing self changed your attitude- and your day around. Practical intelligence helped you. You started living, rather than blaming.

Or perhaps, you were running late for work, the traffic was heavy, the lights were all red, and there a major accident occurs up in front. You were directing your attitude to connect all of these — independent basically neutral events- into a theme of "the world's out to get me — all of these things shouldn't be happening on the same day. I can't take anymore or I'm going to scream!"

In this instance you asked your attitude to go into a blame mode, "If only it weren't for…!"

At that moment of blaming, you gave your power away and the worst consequences were not on the outside world, but on your inside world. The decision was not an intelligent one.

Think of your one self having two components, (1) you as director, and (2) your attitude, your employees (your thoughts, your emotions, & your actions) who you are directing.

You, as director, are your conscious, determining self. Conscious, directing you chooses, and decides, which course for your attitude to take.

Your attitude cannot choose. Your attitude makes your conscious choices happen. When you tell your attitude that something is impossible, or frustrating or shouldn't be, your subconscious, compliant attitude directs its resources-thoughts, emotions and actions into building a stronger case to support your conscious, directing choice. Again, can you remember a time you directed your attitude to go that way?

When you tell your attitude that even though the odds are against us, if we put everything together, we can do anything, your attitude responds with renewed motivation. It is vital to be aware that you choose your attitude. Can you remember a time that you directed your attitude to go this way? It worked, didn't it? That means you were using your practical intelligence.

TELL YOURSELF, "I AM THE CEO (CENTRAL EXECUTIVE OFFICER) OF MY LIFE"

I direct my employees or my attitude tools

If I direct my attitude tools constructively, the practical results are:

1. **My Thoughts:** What I tell myself, determining my destination & developing a road map to get to my determined destination

2. **My Emotions:** My motivational fuel to keep my energized and inspired to keep going

3. **My Actions:** My vehicle, my body, taking action being fueled by my emotions, following the road

    map to my destination determined by my
thoughts

In this case I am in a fully functioning state. I am using
my practical intelligence.

If however, I allow the outside world, or THE WORLD
to determine MY WORLD by blaming ("If it weren't
for...!"), than I give away my power tools. When I don't use
my practical intelligence and start giving my power away by
blaming, the dynamic looks like this:

1. **My Thoughts:** Blaming, "If it weren't for him, her,
   my boss, my past, the traffic, the weather, the
   President, the economy, my weaknesses, the
   should's and shouldn'ts, things changing so
   much, teenagers, old people, the republican's, the
   democrat's, etc., I could be happy."

2. **My Self-created Emotions:** Pain, anger, hurt,
   revenge, helplessness, etc. (Note that the specific
   emotion is directly determined by our specific
   choice of thoughts we determine. For example, if
   I blame my boss, who I make strong and powerful, than I will be giving myself feelings of helplessness.

3. **My Resultant Actions:** Allowing my vehicle, that
   is, my body to steer off the constructive course to
   a goal, and being re-routed in acting on my blaming behaviors. "I can't reach my goal because of
   this or that reason, and so I have to spend my
   energies taking action, fight, resist, passive-

aggressiveness, getting others involved in my anger against my blaming source, etc.

You might note either way that my day has 60 seconds to a minute, 60 minutes to an hour and 24 hours in it. And I have about 30, 000 of these days of potential in my life. I have to determine how I want to spend them. That is the job of a CEO. A lot rests on my decision to blame, "If it weren't for…!" or to live and create.

YOU ARE THE CEO OF YOUR WORLD; BUT YOU ARE NOT THE CEO OF THE WORLD!

The mistake that people make is that while they, as leaders of their lives, are the determiners of THEIR world, they conclude they should be the determiners of THE WORLD. Their frustrations result from their illogical, irrational, painful, and frankly, crazy attitude that I should control you, and you should act the way I want you to act, rather then the way you want to act. And most people frustrate themselves by believing that events in the universe should go MY WAY, rather than THE WAY they are going.

And when people and events don't act the way I want, I will give away my power and blame them. "If it weren't for you,…!"

This is a book about how to take charge of YOUR WORLD first. The person with a high practical intelligence quotient knows that is the surest, most practical approach to life. And when our world is together, we can go to change

THE WORLD. Rather than letting THE WORLD change YOUR WORLD.

1

UNDERSTANDING

Works Better Than Judging

Do you have any relationships in which you believe that if it weren't for the other person, you could along?

Is it possible the other person feels the same way?

Remember: To the other guy, you're the other guy!

Have you ever tried on someone else's glasses and everything you looked at was blurry? If so, did you tell them that their glasses were wrong and that they should throw their glasses away? And then reassure them you will give them your prescription. Because your prescription works better?

Of course not. You wouldn't even think of judging the view that works best for them. You know that their vision is different than yours. That's why we have more eyeglass businesses than you could ever see in a lifetime. There are a couple of them in most malls alone!

You inherently understand the fact that your prescription works best for your vision.

And their prescription works best for them, for their vision.

And, because of your understanding, you aren't working yourself up over their viewpoint, are you?

In other words, when you understand that the other person naturally has a different viewpoint than you do, and you don't take it personally, it doesn't bother you. You respect their view, even though you know it wouldn't work personally for you.

When you think of things this way, that is, when you understand, you find that it works better for you. When you sense that, you are developing your practical intelligence. Because again, it works better for you to understand the other, than it does to judge the other.

Did you ever judge somebody when they saw things differently on an issue in life's landscape than you did? Did you assume that, because their viewpoint was different than yours, that proves that they were wrong?

- Was judging them effective?

- Did judging them bring you closer together?

- Did your learn new things about their view that you didn't see before?

- Did you understand them better?

- Did you grow?

We grow through our willingness to stop judging and start understanding.

CHOOSING BETWEEN JUDGING AND UNDERSTANDING

Whenever any two people talk, each person is deciding to do one of two things.

1. The first choice is to listen to understand the other person from the other person's vantage point.

2. The second option is to judge the other person from one's own vantage point.

Person A speaks	Person B's choices
	1) Listen to understand What is her view? (perspective taking
	How is she looking at this?
	What is she feeling about

this? (empathy)

or

2) Judge the other from my view

Is she right or wrong? (from my view)

More often than not, when Person B is listening to Person A, Person B is thinking, "is she right?" or "Is she wrong?" What Person B is unaware of when they are judging is that they are thinking, according to me. They think they are judging Person A according to the universal truth. (They are also operating out of the belief, usually inaccurately, that Person A even cares.)

The judge is, in grandiose, but fashion, subconsciously assuming, "I have the full truth, I am the compass, the lighthouse, and I am listening to you for the sake of pointing out to you where you are wrong. Sometimes I don't even have to hear you through all of the way, and will save you words interrupting you in mid-thought. You are lucky to have me around. Plus you will know how far off you are from the truth just by sensing how much your ideas disagree with mine."

In other words, if we disagree, *you* have some work to do. For our relationship to succeed, you need to change. I don't have to change because I am right. I'm surprised and annoyed that you can't see that! As a result, we have "the blaming by judging" phenomena, or "If it weren't for you, we could get along!"

DON'T UNDERSTAND TO BE NICE TO THE "OTHER": UNDERSTAND TO BE NICE TO "YOURSELF"

Shh! The person you disagree with didn't buy this book. You did. So while I love them as a fellow human being, I am here for you. I am not asking that you understand them because you should be nice to them, or because it will improve your relationship, or because it will take the pressure off the relationship, or because they will feel understood.

All I am saying is that the person with practical intelligence listens, rather than judges, because it works better for them. In other words, when you stop judging, and blaming, and instead listen and understand, you begin to grow by realizing their is another vantage point, another set of eyeglasses that can be worn looking at the same old thing. Understanding works better. And yes, understanding is only fair.

IMAGINE THE SUPREME COURT HEARING ONLY ONE SIDE OF THE STORY

Why am I so right, and you so wrong when we disagree? Why am I so convinced of the superiority of my position? Very simply, because I live from my vantage point twenty-four hours a day.

For example, I think I have the toughest job because I know intimately all of the stresses my job has. The lazy people in the other department that are holding things up don't have the stress I have, and so I judge them and blame them. This causes resentment and anger in me. I spend most of my day thinking about my job pressure, and very little time thinking about theirs. (Unfortunately the other side is as biased as I am, and is doing the same to me.)

What if the Supreme Court of the United States of America took the same prejudiced, biased position. Imagine if one day the Chief Justice concluded, "I only need to hear one side of the story, and then I'll make my decision."

The outcry would be like an explosion. "This is America, you need to hear both sides of the story. This in unfair!"

When we judge without giving another person equal time to present their viewpoint, we are like the judge who won't give equal time. If we spend twenty-four hours a day focusing on our side, wouldn't it be fair to just use twelve hours and give the other twelve?(And wouldn't the things we learn in the twelve hours they are talking be more informative and helpful to us than the things we learn from the twelve hours we are talking?)

Plus, when we judge, we are violating another great American time-honored principle. We are operating out of the idea that the other person is guilty until proven innocent!

IS IT POSSIBLE THAT THERE IS
ANOTHER VIEWPOINT THAN MY OWN?

Draw a capital letter "E." From one viewpoint, it is clearly an E.

But from other view points, we can see that it could be a W or an M, or even a bad comb. Now which viewpoint it is, depends upon one's point of view.

Can you agree with this? The person who looks to understand fully the alternate possibilities in that letter has the richest view of them all. This person can see more. This as an example of practical intelligence.

Is it possible that the person who listens to understand another's viewpoint is more enriched and grows more, while the judge only goes back to their neighborhood view and continues blaming.

One very interesting experience I had was to work with a school district where conflict was deep. Almost all sides judged, blamed and even hated the other sides because of the judging and blaming. Working with each group for three hours, I asked them to share their viewpoint of the job stresses.

The school board members told me they have to get elected, they are scrutinized by the community, their children are put down by teachers because of the low pay raise, the angry letters they receive from the taxpayers, etc. In three hours time, my own eyes were opened. I had no idea of the depth, importance and stress of their work. In fact I left the meeting concluding that they actually have the toughest job in the school district. I changed my view through understanding. You might say I saw the E like a W.

Then for three hours I worked with school administrators, and I opened myself up to listen to understand their viewpoint. When they told me about dealing with angry parents who only want the most popular teachers for their children, dealing with drug related problems, breaking up fights, and angry teachers, as well as tough school board members, my eyes were again opened. I left this meeting thinking that this group has the toughest job in the district.

Next I met with teachers, and in three hours of understanding, I had the same experience of deep respect. This was followed by meetings with cafeteria workers, bus drivers, custodians, students and parents. Wow, none of this was easy for anyone.

My final meeting was with parents who the teachers said butt in too much, and a parent asked me, "Since we are paying for all of this don't you think we have any rights?"

You see, having been a teacher, I intimately knew the teachers' views on all of the other groups. The blaming, the anger, the division. But now, I had a richer view. I could see things and understand things that at one time I just judged before. This was good for me. It was therapeutic for me. The value of listening to understand is not only to help on the other person. The value of understanding is on me. Because when I stop blaming and start understanding, my life changes.

Oh, back to the school district. How did we resolve the conflict? By bringing everyone together, I spoke to them about what I learned. As each clique sat together, I brought to them my insight about how much they have in common.

"I have had the opportunity to walk a mile in the shoes of everyone here in the school district and I have found that everyone in this room has so much in common."

(They looked at each other with an expression that suggested their collective sentiment that "this guy has really missed the point.")

I continued, "What you have in common is that no matter what you do here in this school district, you have concluded that your group got the raw deal, and all of the other groups have it made."

"This is natural because you spend twenty-four hours a day thinking about your job, and very little on the jobs of your fellow community members who play a different role on your team. You then judge and blame, and this gives you further evidence of your already drawn conclusion. Then perhaps you hang out with people who do the same things that you do, and have the same view as yours, and this gives you even further support. And then you go home at night and share your view with your spouse. His or her only source of input is your view, and he or she is ready to fight for you."

"There is an answer. Spend equal time on the other side of the story. You spend too much time getting a one-sided view. Reach out to listen to understand rather then to judge and blame. This will help the healing."

"And one final thing. Don't understand to help the other person. Understand because it will help you."

THE NEGATIVE OUTCOMES OF BLAMING

When Person B judges instead of understands, Person A's message, Person B may cut off a lot of potentially valuable and honest information. This is information from which Person B can learn, but the person misses the learning opportunity. Let's consider a number of disadvantages when we judge, rather than listen to understand another.

1. We miss some information

2. We frustrate the other person, who is unable to communicate the desired message to us without our judgmental interference.

3. We receive a distorted message, minus details that the speaker believes we don't want to hear, or we can't handle.

4. We hear inaccurate information because the other person tells us what he or she believes we want to hear.

5. We anger the other person when we judge, because he or she feels we are condescending, judgmental and paternal.

These are just a few of the many, many deleterious effects of choosing to judge and blame, rather than to listen to understand another. No wonder a person who seeks to understand, a rare but valued phenomena, becomes more effective with people. Communication with a person who sensitively understands becomes cleaner, clearer, honest and enjoyable.

UNDERSTANDING DOESN'T MEAN AGREEING

Some people make the error of concluding that because they are listening to understand someone, that means they are agreeing with them. Nothing is further from the truth. Non-judgmental listening is one process that focuses on understanding the other person's *viewpoint from the other person's world*. Judging involves listening to the other person to *understand the other person from the judge's world*. So, we can simultaneously understand another person fully, and disagree with the other person completely.

Non-judgmental listening is neither agreeing nor disagreeing because it is an attempt to hear without the foggy interference of one's own viewpoint. In this way the other person's message becomes more accurate and real.

Please note that while we are uncovering the disadvantages of blaming in this book, because it hurts the blamer, we are not taking a stance against judging. You will learn how to effectively confront people later on our discussion on assertiveness. There is a time for disagreeing. And, at that time for disagreeing, we want to have a clear understanding about what we are disagreeing with. That clear understanding comes through our non-judgmental listening. Plus, when we disagree with a solid understanding of the other person's viewpoint, our assertive communication becomes even more effective.

DE-HUMANIZING IS
A FORM OF JUDGING & BLAMING

"You people in the office have no idea about what's going on in the mill."

"The democrats will raise your taxes every time."

De-humanizing is occurring when we relate to another as if, "I'm a person, you're a thing." We reduce the other person or group to a single feature. For example, "he's the janitor," or "you people in sales are all the same." In de-humanizing, we erroneously conclude that (1) all of them think exactly alike, and (2) the way they think is different and inferior to me.

When two countries are at war, both de-humanize the other by labeling each other which has the effect of making the other less than a person. More like a thing. So you can kill the animal. You can see the connection between judging, blaming and de-humanizing.

De-humanizing is overcome be re-humanizing. Re-humanizing occurs when we, first see the other person as a person, and, then, letting the other person's viewpoint in. Its like thinking, "This person is a person just like me. And like me, this person has some viewpoints of life. It would be helpful to me to listen to understand and to learn about this fellow human's viewpoint. If this other person does the same with me, we can learn from each other."

When the sales people and the accounting people de-humanize each other, "sociopathic salespeople," and "anal bean counters," re-humanization is the answer. The result of re-humanizing would have each concluding that, "true, each of us, one in sales and one in accounting have different responsibilities, but each of us are people who (1) have many things in common with each other, and (2) differ in many ways from those who have the same responsibilities as we do.

In *The Brighter Side of Human Nature*, Alfie Kohn suggests that the way we get beyond isolated group membership and move towards re-humanizing is to conclude:

> *"She may be one of them, but she is mostly (1) a person like me, and (2) an individual, distinct from the others in her group."*

In the process of re-humanizing, the other person becomes a person, like me, a person who I am beginning to understand has viewpoints, ideas and feelings. And we are a step closer to realizing the absurdity of a statement such as, "If it weren't for you, we could get along."

WHAT CAN WE DO TO BUILD MUTUAL UNDERSTANDINGS?

In *On Becoming a Person*, psychologist Carl Rogers points out how judgment is the major obstacle to mutual understand, and then offers a solution to overcome the barrier.

"...the major barrier to mutual interpersonal communication is our very natural tendency to judge, evaluate, approve or disapprove, the statements of the other person or group. Although this tendency to make evaluations is common in almost all interchanges of language, it is very much heightened in those situations where feelings and emotions are deeply involved. So the stronger our feelings, the more likely it is that there will be no mutual element in communication. This tendency to react to any emotionally meaningful statement by forming an evaluation of it from our own point of view is, I repeat, the major barrier to interpersonal communication."

"But, is there any way of solving this problem, of avoiding this barrier? Real communication occurs, and this evaluative tendency is avoided when we listen with understanding. What does this mean? It means to see the expressed idea and attitude from the other person's point of view, to sense how it feels to him, to achieve his frame of reference in regard to the thing he is talking about."

Understanding isn't easy. It isn't for everyone. To truly understand, it has been observed by Alfie Kohn that one needs intelligence, cognitive development, imagination, mental health, flexibility, generosity of spirit, and openness.

But the rewards of understanding build bridges to the rich lands of others, giving us opportunities to see new vistas, so that when we return to our perceptual homeland, we are enriched forever.

SKILLS & STRATEGIES TO UNDERSTAND

Communicating Your Desire to Understand The Other Person

To enrich your life through understanding another, start with a determination inside your heart to create a safe, understanding climate for the other person. And next, and this will be more difficult, is to resist the natural tendency to interrupt, judge and blame.

Show your presence in the relationship. You show your presence when you create an atmosphere in which others feel safe to discuss their concerns. You are present by providing time and by attending to their needs. You show an interest in what concerns them. You are making an unselfish commitment to hear them. Your physical presence involves eye-to-eye contact, warmth and a relaxed, open body posture.

Eye Contact

Effective listeners have the ability to use an ideal amount of eye contact when communicating. What is ideal?

Obviously, too little or no eye contact might be perceived as disinterest. On the other hand, constant staring may be threatening and produce defensiveness in the speaker. The ideal amount is one which you feel comfortable, but few breaks in contact. When you are truly listening, your body confirms that.

Another function of eye contact is to convey your empathy for the other person's concerns. Often when we interrupt people while they are speaking, they lose their train of thought. By conveying through your eyes that you are in touch, you communicate your presence without distracting interruption.

Warmth & Open Body Language

A warm person has natural verbal and body language skills that communicate genuine interest, caring and a safe reception to another person. A warm person (1) centers on the other person's interests, (2) communicates moment-to-moment involvement through their facial expressions, (3) presents oneself with open body language, (4) blocks out all other distractions, and (5) is " with" the other person.

Think of warm people you know and model some of their qualities. Warmth is crucial to the understanding climate.

Listening for the Person's Theme

Effective listening involves a desire to thoroughly understand the theme of the speaker's message. This theme can be understood in a variety of ways. Focus on the speaker's view and feelings, as well as the person's body language.

Listening for the Person's View (Perspective Taking)

Let in the other person's viewpoint. If asking questions let them flow from the thought, how can I get a clearer picture of how she is looking at this issue? What is her perspective? What is her viewpoint? Is there a larger theme here? Then play back to the other person your understanding of their perspective.

"Does it look like this?

"Let me see this clearly."

Listening for the Other Person's Feelings (Empathy)

In addition to understanding the other person's perspective, non-judgmental listening involves a sensitivity to the other person's feelings. Ask yourself, "what is this person feeling about these events and issues?" And then reflect some of those feelings back to check for accuracy.

"Were you excited?"

"Sounds like your feelings were hurt."

Observing the Other Person's Body language

People communicate in many ways. In addition to their words, ideas and feelings, their body language can either support what they are saying is accurate (congruent) or there may be a discrepancy that you observe. For example, someone says, "I am really mad at my boss," while smiling. To truly understand, you want to be fully present, safe, warm, sensitive and in tune with the words and feelings of the other person.

In conclusion, through understanding another person, we begin to sense that he, like me, has a vantage point. And it would be most helpful for me to understand his vantage point, because I will stop judging and start growing. Our task is to understand each other's.

The skills and strategies here are designed to help you to resolve conflicts so that you never cause pain and anger for yourself again with the blaming words, "If it weren't for you, we could get along."

Ask if you can wear the glasses of the person you disagree with, and see how things look. And, if the person doesn't wear glasses, and you do, tell the person to get glasses. Like yours. They can change your life, can't they?

Understanding adds to developing our practical intelligence because we get better results. We can further develop our practical intelligence by stop blaming and making our past powerful. And to, instead focus on living in the present and building our future.

2

LIVING TODAY

Gets Us Over Blaming Yesterday

One of my patients looked at me, with a body language revealing helplessness, and explained, "I've had the worst past you could ever imagine."

I responded, "I'm sorry to hear that you had a very difficult past. But I have some great news for you."

"What?"

"Its over!"

"Your past is over."

In another experience, I wanted to toast our friend for her fortieth birthday, but, in anguish, she declined the toast.

"Don't remind me. I'm the big 4-0!"

"Well, Chrissy," I reasoned, "Imagine if this was your sixtieth birthday instead. How much would you give to go back to your fortieth, which is where you are right now?"

"Hmm, ok."

"But Chrissy, may I remind you of today at forty when you were upset because you wish you were twenty instead? And I remember when you were twenty you were upset, because you wanted to be twenty one."

There is only one practical answer. Wherever you are, be there. And it will never really matter what age you are. After you either, go through a crises, or further your practical intelligence, you will realize this insight. Hopefully, it will be the latter.

ARE YOU MAKING THE MISTAKE OF LIMITING THE VISIONS OF YOUR FUTURE BY THE NARROW EXPERIENCES OF YOUR PAST?

Was there a time you weren't toilet trained? Are you toilet trained today? What if you would have concluded, "I guess I'll never be toilet trained?"

Was there a time you couldn't read nor write? Can you read and write today? What if you would have generalized on that moment in time and concluded, "I guess I'll never be able to read and write?"

Isn't it only logical to assume that some things that you couldn't do yesterday, that you could do today or tomorrow?

How?

By start building your future, and stop blaming your past!

TODAY BEGINS YOUR NEW LIFE

Operate out of your practical intelligence and ask yourself, "Isn't today my best chance to change my life?"

Your practical intelligence will start thinking, and, in a short period of time, rule out both yesterday and tomorrow as being the starting point to the new, unstoppable you. In fact, you can start changing your life by seeing yourself as not a product of your past experiences, but, rather, as a dream-seed for your future achievements. To start looking forward, rather than looking back. To enter this moment, not biased by the weaknesses of your past.

You are not your past, today. Look at a clock and a calendar. Notice that they change every minute, and every day. Your body is constantly in change. In fact, it would be impossible to freeze you in any given moment in time. Time moves on. In reality, your past is over. Your past cannot touch you today, unless you give it power by blaming it.

The only influence that your past has on you is in your perception of your past. Two people who grow up in the same family often have dramatically different views of their family years later, because their perceptions are different. It is not our past, but our view of our past, that affects us. The person who uses their practical intelligence knows that to change our past, we change our view of our past.

But there is a more effective approach.

- Get off our past

- Live in the present to

- build our future.

NOW IS OUR ONLY MOMENT OF POWER

Remember, we have about two and one-half billion moments of potential in our life. Imagine that. Two and one-half billion seconds of potential. Any one of those moments could be life changing. Interestingly, a whole lifetime looks overwhelming to manage. Our past experiences, our present pressures, our future worries, How do we handle it all?

Relax. We don't have to control our whole life in this moment called "now." All we have to do is to get the most out of this moment. Where we are today is the result of the choices we made in our past moments called, "now." Where we will be tomorrow will be the result of the choices we make in this moment now. Think about it:

How much we will weigh on the beginning of next year is related to our choices at mealtimes from now until the new year.

Whether we get a speeding ticket this year is directly related to our choice of speeding or not.

We play a role in our life. And awareness of our power in this moment called now opens up our world. The problem occurs when we don't use up our power by living in our past.

WHAT IS HAPPINESS? PUTTING YOURSELF INTO A STATE OF FLOW!

"Flow," is a word used and written about by Mihaly Csikszentmihalyi in his book of the same name. The author concluded that for 2,300 years, since Aristotle asked the question, "What is happiness?" no answer could be found. But he argues that we now found what happiness is.

Happiness is the state of being totally absorbed in a task. This is when we are in a flow. Flow improves the quality of that experience and provides increased enjoyment, concentration and involvement. In flow, the sense of time and self-consciousness disappears, and a feeling of transcendence and breaking out of boundaries appears.

Flow is the state of being so absorbed in an activity that nothing else seems to matter. The immersion in the experience itself takes the focus away from self-consciousness and outside problems.

Curiously, happiness is not something that happens, nor something that power can command. It does not depend upon outside events, but rather how we interpret them. Happiness is a condition that must be prepared for and cultivated by each of us privately. People who control their inner experiences are those who can determine and enhance the quality of their lives.

PROBLEMS WITH RE-LIVING OUR PAST

As you develop your practical intelligence, it becomes increasingly clear with each lesson that there are many reasons to stop dwelling on the past. Here are three of them. You can add many more.

First when we focus on the past, we use up our power in this now moment with what was rather than what could be. How many of our moments of potential are lost because of wasting our time on what was. I have a good friend. Ed never knew his biological parents and experienced many setbacks in his young life but, self-determined, Ed consciously moved on. Of course he was curious, and of course, he wanted to meet his parents, but he used his time to build his future, not to blame his past.

A second problem associated with re-living the past is that not only does it consume our finite amount of time, but if we find some answers to why we are the way we are today, how do we know for sure? How can we prove that we are afraid of public speaking because our mother was a perfectionist? And so, what if she was a perfectionist. What should we do then, once we gather this "insight?"

Blame our mother? Blame our self? Or move forward?

The third problem with digging up our past, in addition to using up our time that could be creating our future, and the tenuous nature of our insight, is the fact that we now will start to blame the people and experiences of our past for doing these things to us.

"If it weren't for my past, I could have a great future."

STRATEGIES FOR LEAVING THE PAST BEHIND, AND LOOKING FORWARD

Imagine yourself ten years from now talking to yourself today. Think of some current problems you face and ask yourself, that is, your ten year older self, "How should I deal with that situation today, to make it better for you ten years from now?

To maximize your life, the ideal is that you are your best only in one moment. And that moment is now. You can't change your past, but you can sure change your future by acting out of who you want to be, not out of who you were. You can begin now, by becoming aware of the power of this moment.

THE MOST MOVING INSIGHT OF LIFE

In my practice I constantly wondered why some people suddenly, at some moment of personal transformation really begin to understand life. Others never experience that illuminating moment that shapes their new future and lifts them up above their past. Interested in the biographies of successful people, I tried to learn why some made it against all odds, while others let the smallest matters send then living on "The Streets of Past Blames," for the rest of their lives. I thought if we could find the difference, others, who were open-minded and ready to grow could benefit. I think we found it.

THE SUCCESS ATTITUDE: FOCUSING ON WHAT CAN BE, NOT ON WHAT WAS

In observing both unhappy (low developed P.I.) and fulfilled people (high developed P.I.), there is a major difference between the two in another way. The difference is born in that moment when everything becomes clear about one's relationship with life. What separated the most fulfilled and the least fulfilled humans occurred at the instant they realized that:

> *"I am not an effect of my life experiences (Blame)"*

> *"I am the cause of my life experiences (Live)!" (High P.I.)*

Unhappy people inevitably believe that they are an effect, helpless and caused by something over which they have no control, such as their past. The self-actualized person, one who is making more of her possibilities actual, however, thinks, "I cause. I cause how people see me. I cause how I choose to respond to life. I cause myself to set goals for myself. I cause my future. I face challenges and I cause myself not to give up."

BECOMING A FIND-A-WAYER

The world is divided into two kinds of people. Some give up when faced with a barrier. They make excuses, blame their past or other people, find fault with everything. One doesn't have to drive to the library to realize that that just doesn't work. Its not very practical.

Others, faced with the same challenges go on to find a way. That works a lot better. Both have the same amount of time. One life time.

Find-a-wayers operate out of the conviction that problems have solutions The move from the spirit of Winston Churchill who proclaimed, "If my best isn't good enough, I'll do better!" They draw from their unlimited creative determination to overcome their past views, while others search for rationalizations for their failures.

Please note that a rationalization is giving a "good," reason, rather than the "true," reason why we were held back. Explaining that "the sun was in my eyes," appears enough reason for an outfielder to miss the ball and lose the game.

Contrarily a find-a-wayer would have prepared by bringing sunglasses. Rationalizing that one failed to get a promotion because the boss liked someone else better appears to be a good reason, but to a find-a-wayer recognizes that it is important to have good human relations skills, and tact with a boss to gain the boss's trust. They are not aware that all other things being equal, they also would hire the person with whom they feel most comfortable.

10 RATIONALIZATIONS THAT BLOCK OUR POTENTIAL IN THE PRESENT (PAST WAYS OF LOOKING AT THINGS THAT WE STILL ARGUE FOR TODAY)

1. It's never been done before. Or I've never done it before.

2. If only I had this one other thing, I could do the job.

3. The economy is bad.

4. It's my age. I'm not the right age for that.

5. I don't have any luck. I can't get a break.

6. I don't have the education background in my past.

7. I'm not big enough.

8. I could fail. I tried it before and it didn't work.

9. My health is poor. I'm handicapped.

10 Other people do things like that. Not me.

Let's explore each of these rationalizations and see how they are interpreted differently by find-a-wayers.

1   Instead of the rationalization, "It's never been done before," or "I've never done it before," the find-a-wayer concludes, "I'm not going to limit the visions of my future by the narrow experiences of my past." The find-a-wayer knows that almost everything we see in the world at one time wasn't here, and had to be done a first time. In fact, almost everything that you as a human being can do today, you couldn't do in your past. There had to be a first time. The moment that you realize that you are a cause, and not an effect, a mental barrier opens up and gives way to a ceilingless sky of potential.

In their popular book, **Mind Power**, Bernie Zilbergeld and Arnold Lazarus wrote:

"Before May 6, 1954, no one had ever run a mile under four minutes; lots of runners had tried and many had come close, but there was a barrier. Many runners and scholars argued that the barrier was physiological, that human bodies simply couldn't run that fast. As Roger Bannister, the first human to break the barrier, said, 'Everyone used to think it was quite impossible and beyond the reach of the runner.' But Bannister never thought this himself and prepared himself accordingly. What is perhaps even more aston-

ishing than Bannister's own achievement is that once he proved that it could be done, others were also able to do it. By now hundreds and hundreds of runners have run a mile in less than four minutes. It is doubtful that human physiology underwent a significant change in that period. What is far more likely is that before Bannister's accomplishment, the self-limiting notion that the four minute mile was impossible made it impossible. Once Bannister proved it was possible, something changed in the minds of the other runners."

"A similar thing happened in weightlifting. Before Vasily Alexeev lifted 501 pounds in 1976, no one had ever lifted 500 pounds over his head, and many argued that it was a physiological impossibility. But in the month after Alexeev broke the barrier, four other weight lifters lifted over 500 pounds. By now scores have done it. Why? The analysis of Arnold Schwarznegger is undoubtedly correct. 'They believed it was now possible. The body didn't change that month. How could the body change that much? It was the same body, but the mind was different. Mentally it's possible to break records. Once you understand that, you can do it.'"

My friend Leif Cook, the Scandinavian entrepreneur, talks about the impossible this way, "If something is possible, it's already done. If something is impossible, let's begin to do it." Henry Ford told us, "Believe you can or believe you can't; either way'll you'll be correct. And philosopher Baruch Spinoza urged us mentally over our past when he concluded, "For as long as you believe that something is impossible, for that exact period of time it will be impossible." And we add, "The moment you see that challenge as being reachable, that is the very moment you go on to conquer the challenge."

In speaking to an Ohio graduating class, I asked the cap and gown seniors, "Who in here believes that we can cure the world's hunger problems in the next five years? Not one of them raised their hands. And I responded, "That's why we won't, because we have already drawn a conclusion in our heads about the impossibility of the challenge. The world needs just one of you in this room to raise your hands to get our hope started. And to stop making the mistake of limiting the visions of our future by the narrow experiences of our past."

2 In lieu of the second rationalization that, "if only I had this one other thing, I could succeed," the find-a-wayer looks inside his or her creative mind. A peppy young college girl named Carol Johnston set herself a goal of becoming a gymnast on a university team. Less the five feet tall, she faced a barrier, having only one arm. For a gymnast! Yet she didn't spend her time excusing,

rationalizing or blaming. Carol set her will compass on a course for success, and worked harder. The petite mountain of inspiration concluded that having only one arm meant she had to find a way by working harder than anyone else. Her mind made up for what was missing in her body.

Competing against hundreds of other girls with both arms, she made the U.C.L.A. gymnastic team. Her success story did not end there. Carol became one of the top gymnasts in the world! Often the only missing part for finding the way to our dreams is in our mind.

3   The rationalization that, "I can't succeed because of the economy," is inferior to the view that, "I, not the economy, decide my next move." In his important book, *The Magic of Getting What You Want*, Davis Schwartz wrote, "Huge, prosperous businesses such as McDonalds, Ford, Kentucky Fried Chicken were started by people with very little capitol. Furthermore, all except for two of the people who led the United States, Hoover, Truman, Eisenhower, Johnson, Nixon, Ford, Carter, Reagan and Clinton were born to poor or moderately well off parents.

Often the economy doesn't destroy a business, but the attitudes that people develop about a downhill economy lead them to act in ways to cause defeat and create a self-fulfilling prophecy of failure. A friend of mine had a successful sandwich shop in a small Pennsylvania town. In addition to the economy slipping at the time, a big restaurant opened across the street. My friend was defeated in his mind weeks before the other restaurant opened its door. When the restaurant finally opened in a short while he was telling me about the customers he was losing. They were going, "across the street." As we talked, he began to realize how his defeatist attitude was causing his business failure.

"You see, Lew, I knew the economy was getting bad, and then that new restaurant opened; so I immediately started cutting back on orders to prepare for the slowdown. For the last few days, in fact, I haven't had any bread or rolls left for sandwiches in the evening. As you can suspect, even some of my regulars started going over there because I couldn't give them what they wanted."

I asked my gloomy friend, "Wait a second. Are you saying that you cut back in orders because somehow or other you knew that your competition would take away your regulars? And while they were still coming to you, you couldn't serve them so that they had to go across the street?"

"Yes."

"Well, perhaps that suggests that you better take a clearer look at your future in a more positive way and increase your orders so that a customer will never have to leave disappointed. Perhaps now, in this economy, is the time to start offering specials and taking advantage of all the new traffic that your competition is bringing into the area. Don't defeat yourself by blaming the economy. Let the economy, whether it be positive or negative, work in your favor. Don't accept the rationalization of the economy."

To a find-a-wayer, ideas and creativity are more important than money. The only value of money is that it enables you to find and hire find-a-wayers.

4 Find-a-wayers don't lean on the excuse of age, and reject the "I'm not the right age," rationalization. Can you imagine someone finding a cure for a common cold, and having people with colds asking the question, "How old is the discoverer?" Age is a rationalization that blocks the go forward spirit. Theodore Roosevelt, John Kennedy, and Bill Clinton were in their early 40's when they became Presidents of the United States. Dwight Gooden was 20 when he was the best pitcher in baseball. Michael Dell was in fourth grade when he applied to take his high school equivalency test. Numerous high tech businesses were built

by entrepreneurs who became millionaires in their early 20's.

By the same token, "too old," has been another historic excuse for not trying. As I watched Grandma Hilda on TV, at ago 92, on top of Japan's largest mountain, and heard her say, "This sort of climb keeps you young," my eyes were opened to the possibilities of an inspired human, at any age. Colonel sanders founded Kentucky fried Chicken after he was retired.

David Schwartz puts the question of being too old in its real perspective in his book, ***The Magic of Thinking Big***. After a training session, a man told Dr. Schwartz that he was thinking of a career change, but he would have to start from scratch. At his age, 40, it would be quite difficult. Schwartz asked the man when he thought a person's productive years began, they agreed at around age 20. They also agreed that even very conservatively speaking, one's productive years end at age 70. Schwartz pointed out that there are fifty years of productivity in a person's life. The man, at age 40, had used up only 20 of his fifty years. He still had thirty years or sixty per cent of his productive years left. And he was afraid of making a change!

Psychiatrist Alfred Adler was once told by a middle aged person, "I'm too old to go to school because if I start today, it will be four years until

I earn the degree." Adler responded, "And, if you start tomorrow, it will be four years and a day."

It is the rare person who, underneath, doesn't harbor the excuse of inappropriate age. How many people actually do feel they are at, just the right age? What is the right age?

Any age is right, and no age is more right than the age you are... today. You have never had so much experience, and you will never be younger than you are today!

5 Instead of the rationalization that "I don't have any luck," or, "I can't get a break," find-a-wayers don't wait for breaks and luck. They believe that highly motivated, persistent people attract good luck and get the breaks. While writing a book, **Think Your Way To Success**, I did some research to uncover whether there was a difference between the ways successful and unsuccessful people viewed the role of luck in their lives. I encourage you to try the same experiment.

First, identify five people in your life who you consider happy and successful. Then compose a list of five people whom you consider less than successful, and down on life. Ask all ten people the same question.

Ask the people in your survey this question: "How much of a role do you believe that luck plays in your life? Then record all ten answers so that you can scientifically analyze patterns in their responses, if any. If you find that the five you identified as successful have a different pattern in their responses from the other five, you may have discovered a view present that has a huge consequence on success.

Until you get your results, allow me to share some of the responses I received from my interviews. First, the unhappy group:

"Luck is everything. You just have to be at the right place, at right time." (male, age 27, unemployed for three and one-half years. He has not filled out a job application for two years, and lives with his parents.)

"The cards of life are stacked against you if you don't have money." (female, 36, former sales woman who recently lost her position because of poor sales performance and missed appointments.)

"Some people just get all of the breaks in life." (male 19, recent college dropout)

As you analyze these three responses, you'll notice that each gives luck the key role in determining success. They just were not lucky, and didn't get the breaks, have the money or know the right people. Next, here are some responses that I classified as happy, successful and in charge of their lives.

"You make your own luck." (female, age 32, recently received an award for being one of the top ten teachers in the State of Pennsylvania.)

"It wasn't luck that I haven't missed a single sales appointment in the last two years. It wasn't luck that I made sure that every single order I received from customers was promptly filled. It wasn't luck that I made it my business to take at least four sales training or motivation courses every year. It wasn't luck that I went back to school in the evenings and in less than eight years earned a bachelor's degree in business. Come to think of it, it wasn't luck that my shoes were shined and my shirts were spotless when I made my sales calls. No, it wasn't luck that made me the top sales man last year. And, it won't be luck when I do it again this year." (male, 39, top salesman)

My favorite response came from an author of fiction books. He described how early in life he was discouraged from a career in writing by failure centered thinkers who told him that it was impossible to get a book published unless you either had a lot of money or an, "in." His response to the question asking his thoughts on the role of luck on success:

"I concluded that waiting for luck to come to me before I did something myself was like looking into the mirror at my reflection and waiting for my reflection to move first. There is a more effective way. When I move, my reflection will passively follow. Everytime."

The attitudes of successes and failures became clear to me, and, I trust, will become clear to you when you analyze the results of your interviews. Failures tend to believe that people become successful because of things outside themselves. Thus, they wait, wish and hope for the break. And then, when it doesn't come, they rationalize, excuse and blame.

Successful people, contrarily, tend to see achievement as a product of personal effort. And, if there is such a thing as luck, then, highly motivated, persistent people are the ones who, in the long run, tend to attract it. As one philosopher concluded, "The best winds seem to favor the best sailors."

6 While rationalizers stop themselves from forward progress because of not having the right background, find-a-wayers believe the "backbone is more important than backbone." Rationalizers look into the past to see what is missing and give up because of it, find-a-wayers view of the same

situation is, "I am determined to learn whatever I need to learn to reach my goal. I may have to work a little harder because I don't have the formal background, but that doesn't matter. With determination, I will compensate."

President Truman, whom some regard as one of the gutsier U. S. Presidents might not have run for the highest office in the land because he had a only a high school education. That didn't stop him and he learned what he had to learn to get the presidency.

Albert Einstein, rather than giving up after failing physics, plowed forward to learn everything he could on his own. His insights changed the world, and it is the physics understood by Einstein that the world now studies.

Thomas Edison, perhaps the greatest inventor the world has known, quit school at age 8. He sold newspapers on a street corner, and by age 9 had sub-contracted his paper route to a younger child so that he could spend each day in the Detroit Library. The light bulb, phonograph, curling iron and synthetic rubber are just a few of his more than thousand inventions.

My friend Ed Rose enjoyed going to the great annual highly informative conference conducted by The University of North Texas Center for the Study of Work Teams. He had a message to deliver. He was asked if he was a university graduate and if he had written any books, like the other presenters. He did neither, but his heart guaranteed that Ed's future would be brighter than his past. He enrolled at a Florida University, wrote a half dozen books, and like magic, you can see him passionately conducting a workshop at the September Conference. Ed is also the Worldwide Training Manager of the huge Intersil Corporation. Don't tell Ed your background is holding you back unless you are ready for a twenty-four hour motivation session.

Another good buddy, and my personal role model, is Tom Chlebos, one of S.C.Johnson Wax's leaders who helped transform the great family owned company into a work team environment. A tough job, changing the way people go to work. But Tom and his team learned everything they could about teams, and through his winning personality and his knowledge, today, the company steeped in a hundred year philosophy of believing in people, is truly living its dream. And, in his modest way, Tom, sitting in the background spends his time giving credit to others. Tom had to learn all about teams, and today is one of the leading experts, in the world, on creating a team-based work environment.

Avoid the rationalization of not initially having the background knowledge and remember the examples of Truman, Einstein, Edison, Ed Rose and Tom Chlebos. Simply become determined to learn everything you need to know to reach your dream. The library door of life is always opened for the determined person.

7
The "I'm not big enough," rationalization is easily overcome with the realization that, "Physical size is one thing, but visionary stature is another, related only to the depths of one's mind." Find-a-wayers don't let their current size affect who they will be in the future.

In the early 1900's, the National Football League was founded. A little city called, Green Bay, Wisconsin formed a team. The city had less than 20,000 people, but its size in thinking was equal to New York's, Boston's, and Chicago's. By 1957, the team moved from playing at the high school stadium with 58,000 seats, for a population of only 63,000. Big thinking. Every game was sold out, and a few years later the little city of Green Bay proudly won its first Super Bowl game.

At five feet five inches, Spud Webb is the shortest basketball player in the pro's, and he can dunk a basketball. Size of vision is what counts. Don't be intimidated by the big competitors. Think big. And, remember, size is related to just one thing, and depth of the vision in your mind.

There will never be a better time for you then right now!

8 Rationalizers don't act because they are afraid that they might fail. Find-a-wayers believe that one fails only by failing to act. Find-a-wayers believe that, "I could never fail because no matter what happens when I act, I get knowledge, feedback and information that makes me better equipped for the future."

Remember, you cannot fail. When you act, you receive knowledge, feedback and results. When you fail to act, you fail to get information you can use for your future.

9 Rationalizing that "My health is poor, so I can't succeed," gives way to the find-a-wayer's conviction that, "Although my health may not allow me to do some things, that doesn't mean I can't do anything. There are many things I can do and I will excel at them."

I'll never forget an incident that happened a few years ago as handicapped children were getting on a school bus for the first day of school. A helpful woman tried to assist a teenager up the steps. Politely, he turned to her and said, "Thanks anyway, but I can see and I can walk. I have a hearing problem, but everything else I can do." The kind woman made the mistake of generalizing from a single problem to a general problem.

We all tend to make the same mistakes at times, thinking that because we can't do one thing as a result of health issues, that we can't do anything at all. Nothing could be farther from the truth.

President Eisenhower and Johnson had heart attacks, as did Vice President Cheney, but that didn't stop them from reaching for their dreams.

Helen Keller inspired us that, "one can not consent to creep when one has the impulse to soar."

Ray Charles and Stevie Wonder learned to see with their fingers, their ears, and their hearts. Stevie Wonder even wrote a song describing the birth of his little girl, "Isn't she lovely?"

10

Rationalizers think that other people, not people like them do great things. Find-a-wayers know that "great things are achieved by humans, just like me, who have an extraordinary determination to surmount any obstacle and the creative determination to find a way." Remember most people make two mistakes, overestimating others and underestimating themselves.

The truth is that when you lift your chin of determination, and you have a passionate purpose in life, you have what you need.

LIVE TODAY: USE THIS MOMENT AS AN END IN ITSELF

Imagine. Some students take a college course to get a degree to graduate to get a good job to retire early. Most of our lives we are doing something now because it will lead to a reward that we will receive later. When you think about it then, most of our valuable two and one-half billion moments of life are lost and consumed as mere moments to serve another end. Another moment later, sometimes in the future, will be the rewarding one.

When we are living this powerful moment called now fully, we are creating more rewarding moments for ourself. The college student taking the science course puts their heart into the course, and "flows" and enjoys today's course as an end in itself. Not as a means to a good grade.

IT DOESN'T MATTER WHERE YOU HAVE BEEN IT ONLY MATTERS WHERE YOU ARE GOING

No one has had a perfect past. Everyone can find a problem with this or that. The rich look back and experience their loss of privacy, their distrust of being valued for their money, rather than for themselves. The poor focus on all of the things they didn't have. Everybody has a strong argument to feel shorted. This book is not designed to further those arguments, but to say, What is the most practical thing that we can do - rich or poor, privileged or deprived, to move ourself foreword.

The answer never lies in what was, but rather in what will be. Get the momentum started in your own life. Build your practical intelligence and go forward. Tomorrow you will be further than today. See what's right with you, rather than what's wrong with you. That is the bright way of looking at things because that will make your future brighter. And fill your present up with possibilities.

3

POSITIVE FOCUSING

*Strengthens More Than Blaming
Our Weaknesses*

WE SEE MORE OF WHATEVER
WE FOCUS ON

The next time you are in a room full of people, pick a color that you see in the room. For example, imagine if you choose the color red. Look more closely around you and try to isolate everything that is red. Red sweaters, dresses, ties, carpets, drapes, coke cans, etc. Take a minute or so and bring everything into the foreground with red focusing.

You soon will notice things, that are red, that you didn't notice before. The red may even appear like it is reaching out to you. Maybe the room even looks like it is dominated by red things. Every other color starts to become insignificant, just blending into the background.

Now, close your eyes and erase your red focusing. When you open your eyes again, choose another color to give your perceptual power away to.

Focus on, say white. Bring everything white strongly into the foreground. Soon you will see more white than you ever dreamed was in the room. Slowly, red, and all of the other colors, fade into the background.

One of the fastest ways to change your world is to change your focusing. What you focus on, you begin to see more of.

SEE NEGATIVES IN PERSPECTIVE

While in a taxi en route to speaking to students in an Omaha school, I told the driver I was going to be working with teenagers.

Bitter, he argued, "Teenagers, I'll tell you about teenagers."

He pulled out the Omaha newspaper and threw the headlines to me.

"Look at that!"

"Two Omaha Boys Caught Starting a Warehouse Fire," the headlines read.

"That's what we have in teenagers!" he added.

I asked him how many teenagers were in all of Omaha.

Obviously uninformed he replied, "About 40,000."

"Wow," I returned, "if I was the editor of today's newspaper, the headlines would have read, "Rejoice- 39,998 or 99.99+% of Omaha Children Not Caught Starting Warehouse Fires!"

What do you want to build your own life philosophy on—the 39,998 or the 2? While both are facts, which one is more common? Obviously, there are many times more children who are responsible. Both newspapers and many, everyday conversations focus on the rare, which is the negative.

Once we decide to focus on what's right or what's wrong, we will immediately begin seeing more of what we chose to look for. And obviously, you can see the tremendous advantage an optimist has over a pessimist. They both see whatever they look for.

THE DIFFERENCE BETWEEN BLAMING OURSELVES AND TAKING RESPONSIBILITY

When we stop blaming others, instead of judging them, we sensitively listen to them, to understand them more effectively, from their vantage point. But, in the process, we are not blaming ourself for blaming others. In other words, we are taking responsibility to change our behavior, not blaming ourself (If it weren't for me being a blamer, we could get along!")

Or, when we take responsibility for our life today, rather than living in the past, we are moving forward without blame. Blaming is unproductive and is the accompanying thought, "If it weren't for me for being so rotten and dwelling on the past, I could get ahead. Its all my fault."

In blaming, we are actually blaming ourself for holding us back. "We could be so much better if it weren't for ourself!"

Self-blamers put the blame for their behavior on themselves as opposed to holding themselves responsible. When people take the blame for their behavior, it is just as unproductive as placing the blame on external factors. Blame is a moral judgment and tends to a lead to a negative personal evaluation, but no change in actions.

Taking responsibility, rather than self-blame is more productive. When people take personal responsibility, they act courageously, and are not immobilized by their own worthlessness. But self blamers are so filled with blame, guilt, shame and doubt that they use all of their energies blaming themselves and have no energies left to get out of their self-created ruts. So, whereas self-blame results in self-pity, personal responsibility results in actions and change.

Self-blamers, in a curious way, have a real luxury. After all, if they feel guilty, they don't have to change. Surely just feeling guilty should be suffering enough, they reason. Should they feel weak, someone strong will come along, and take on their responsibility.

Self-blamers wallow in rejection. They feel that their worth has been attacked, and they chooses immobility. Self-responsible, courageous people are concerned about increasing their skills. They learn from situations. They use their energies to develop a more constructive plan rather than swim in self-defeating emotions. They are active and responsible, whereas self-blamers are passive and irresponsible.

TAKE TODAY TO REALIZE
WHAT IS RIGHT WITH YOU

Most people are more talented at seeing their shortcomings and limitations than is seeing their assets, strengths, resources and potential. They don't realize that if they have strengths and aren't aware of those positive qualities, they are fooling themselves. Don't lie to yourself. The world needs you to be your best. What is right with you.

Sit back for a few minutes, play some relaxing music, or go to a peaceful setting and ask yourself each of the following ten questions. After brainstorming with yourself following each question, jot in your impressions on a paper for you to keep for the rest of your life.

1

What are some of the things I accomplished that has given me personal satisfaction?

Some areas you might include are:

- school accomplishments, including particular subjects

- social accomplishments, like helping a friend through a tough time, or inspiring someone to believe in herself

- parental achievements

- athletic achievement

- personal challenges

- physical successes, like losing weight

- professional successes

- spiritual development

Think about these in time lines:

Ages 0-9 _____
_____
_____

10-19 _____
_____
_____

20-29 _____
_____
_____

30-39 _____
_____
_____

40-49 _____
_____
_____

50-59 _____
_____
_____

60-69 _____
_____
_____

70+ _____
_____
_____

2 What do I consider to be my five most important assets? (Don't move on until you have found at least 5)

a. _____
_____
_____

b. _____
_____
_____

c. _____
_____
_____

d. _____
_____
_____

e. _____
_____
_____

3   Think of the 5 people who I respect the most in
    the world. What do I have in common with each?

a. _____
   _____
   _____

b. _____
   _____
   _____

c. _____
   _____
   _____

d. _____
   _____
   _____

e. _____
   _____
   _____

4

Think of 5 things I have done for other people
that were really helpful to them at the time.

a. _____
_____
_____

b. _____
_____
_____

c. _____
_____
_____

d. _____
_____
_____

e. _____
_____
_____

5

What are the 3 best things I have that I can give in a personal relationship?

a. _____
_____
_____

b. _____
_____
_____

c. _____
_____
_____

d. _____
_____
_____

e. _____
_____
_____

6 To whom could I really give a boost today by giving a surprise call?

_____
_____
_____
_____

7 What was the thing in my life that I wanted the
most, worked hard at and finally achieved it?
Recall the experience, and then list the 3 top positive qualities it took for me to achieve that goal?

a. _____
_____
_____

b. _____
_____
_____

c. _____
_____
_____

8   When did I fail at something, and then, through my determination, fight back and overcome the failure? As I relive the experience, what are the 2 most important qualities did it take for me to come back?

a. _____
   _____
   _____

b. _____
   _____
   _____

9   Can I remember a time when my attitude was the difference in the situation? Remember the situation and recall me talking to my attitude. What did I tell my attitude that eventually changed it, and helped me through the situation?

_____
_____
_____
_____

10

What trait would I like to develop today?
Go over my list of my previous 9 questions,
gain strength from it and ask my attitude to
help me bring out this trait that I desire since it is
inside me.

_____

_____

_____

_____

_____

GETTING ENTHUSED ABOUT YOURSELF, AND YOUR UNIQUENESS

You are, literally a miracle. You are such a rare combination of the physical and spiritual, that there is no one, any where in the world, exactly like you. You are so special that you have been given the greatest gift in the world. You were selected to be a human being. You are the owner of your body, your mind, your actions, your thoughts, your feelings, and your attitude. Even your dreams are uniquely yours. And this is your moment in the history of our universe. You are alive, and this gives you the power to draw up the blueprints for the kind of person you want to be.

Tap those human powers you have by igniting the power of enthusiasm for yourself and your possibilities. In fact, you are your possibilities in the beginning stages just waiting to happen. Your success happens when you flash a light on what's right with you. You can start by becoming enthusiastic and let it show.

To become enthusiastic:

Smile enthusiastically. Wherever you go watch the life giving power your smile has on people. Ask people the question, "Who would you rather be with, an enthusiastic person, or a person with a frown?" No surprise to you I'm sure that not one single person chose the frown. Be the energy wherever you go. Even if it seems unnatural to at first extend a warm, welcoming smile to everyone, it will soon be as natural to you as tying your shoes. To realize the power of a smile just think of two people.

The first person who never smiles, we'll call I. M. Dull. How do you feel around I. M. Dull? Would you be likely to buy something from I. M. Dull? Would you enjoy listening to I. M. Dull?

Now consider another person, a good listener who meets you with a warm smile. Let's call this person N. Thusiastic. N. Thusiastic listens to you, gets excited about the things that interest you and is very respectful and positive. Doesn't this person give you more life than I. M. Dull? Be determined that you will use your self-determined resource, your attitude and translate your positive attitude to your life and go forward in the world with a big smile. It will give you a huge advantage.

Walk enthusiastically. Enthusiasts walk faster. Why not? They are going places. Compare the walks of I. M. Dull and N. Thusiastic. While Dull walks with head down, shoulders curved inward, and with a short, apologetic step, N. Thusiastic walks with head up (even in the rain), shoulders back and has crisp gait. Without even meeting these two people, you draw conclusions about them, just by observing their walks. Their walks tell a story. Interestingly, research demonstrates that most of the victims of muggings tend to have a certain walk. Prisoners who were serving time for muggings agreed that a person's walk strongly influenced their decision to attack. The person most likely to become a mugging victim is taking short, shuffling steps with the chest buried between the shoulders. Remember, your walk stems from your self-image, but your self-image can be enhanced from how you walk. Change the way you walk, like N. Thusiast and soon the world will see that you are going places, but more importantly, you will feel yourself getting places faster. Win people over even before you meet them by your confident, enthusiastic walk.

Get psyched on yourself by speaking enthusiastically. Modulate your voice. Every person can remember never ending sermons in church given by a monotonous speaker. Yet, the same words brought to life by an enthusiastic speaker can give energy to the group and make the talk even more powerful. You remember teachers, as well, who brought their lessons to life. Or perhaps you experienced a sales person who went on to simply describe a house, a car or even furniture with no life. The enthusiast puts vitality in the talk. Hold people's attention by putting refreshment in everything you say. Say, "Hello!' with meaning. Say, "Congratulations," with thrill. Say, "Have a great day!" with belief and enthusiasm.

When you vitalize things, something interesting happens. You actually invigorate yourself. When someone asks you how you are doing, do you just say, "OK," or even more helplessly, "Awful," or do you respond with an energetic, "I'm turbo charged!" By enlivening your responses, you are lifted. Remember your words are emotional triggers to your attitude. Watch what you say.

Never say anything that you don't want to be realized. Remember, you are the director of your attitude tools- your thoughts, your emotions and your actions. When you put yourself down, your attitude follow your advice.

"I could never do well in a math class."

"I'm no good at selling."

Your attitude is your servant. And when you direct it into a negative direction, it will go, and use its massive resources of thoughts, emotions and actions and bring you back the results you requested.

That is why speaking enthusiastically, telling yourself things like "This is going to be a great day," triggers your attitude to use its tools to make it a positive day for you.

Use a vocabulary filled with enthusiastic words. More and more psychological research is demonstrating the power of words on a person's emotions. If you think of it, down and out people tend to have a vocabulary filled with gloomy, inactive and depressing words. Contrarily, enthusiastic people tend to use words that are overflowing with positive, uplifting, active, and if need be, assertive words. Two prominent behavioral scientists, Albert Ellis and Robert Harper, co-authors of *A New Guide to Rational Living* and Charles Zastrow, author of *Talk to Yourself* demonstrate how we create our emotions by the words we use. Uplift your life by uplifting the words you use.

Compare the words of our friends
I. M. Dull and N. Thusiastic:

Failure vs. Success Vocabulary

I. M. Dulls says	N. Thusiastic says
"Things are awful, terrible"	"We face an exciting challenge"
"I hate aging"	"I love aging. Consider the option"
"I'm too old to change"	"My experiences give me an advantage"
"Maybe it can be done"	"Knowing us, we can do it"
"Things are OK"	"Things are great"
"Let's give up. Its no use"	"Let's put ourselves into second gear"
"Good job"	"Fantastic performance"

Like N. Thusiast, build your self on a foundation of strong, positive words. If you do, you'll notice your emotions change before your very own eyes. And more importantly, you will be realizing your tremendous power to direct and control your attitude, which means your life.

Wake up enthusiastically. In the morning, while most people treat their alarm clocks like their enemy, look at your alarm clock as though it was a friendly fire alarm. When it rings, jump out of bed fired up with your enthusiasm. Put an immediate, early morning glow in your mind and in your heart. An enthusiastic start to the day gives you an advantage over the ho-hum person who needs an hour, or a morning cup of coffee, or a morning smoke to get going.

Answer your phone enthusiastically. Get off automatic pilot and get enthused every time your phone rings. Remember, the person calling has taken the time to dial you. Let the person catch your enthusiasm right from the start. While the programmed robot says a dull hello, the enthusiast answers with a cheery, "Good morning," or even, "With a little good news from you, both of our days can be improved!"

Your opening words on the phone are only limited by your creativity!

Listen enthusiastically. Win people over by employing the rarely used skill of enthusiastic listening. As you listen to people talk, lean forward. Use open, expressive eyes conveying full attention to the speaker's ideas. The world's best sales people are not only great speakers, but enthusiastic listeners, as well. Stay away from games like, "Can you top this," when listening to another share a proud achievement.

In addition to using your enthusiasm (because it works better than apathy), you can increase your practical intelligence by empowering yourself from drawing from the bigger you.

ACT OUT OF OUR UNLIMITED SPIRIT, NOT YOUR DEFENSIVE EGO

You can put your radio on either AM or FM. Your choice will affect what you hear.

In your everyday life, you can make a similar choice, to either act out of your defensive ego, or out of your unlimited spirit. Our ego is our smallest possible self which gives us very little strength and power to cope with our life challenges. When we act out of our unlimited spirit, we are operating out of our creative resources, as wide as the universe of our minds.

Let's compare the relative capacity, force and vitality present in each of the two extremes.

Ego State	Spirit State
Self-blaming	Inspirational
Threatened	Embraces
Physical Form	Boundless Energies

Limited in Time	Timeless Reference
Limited in Place	Universal
Defends	Creates
Maintenance	Enhancement
Disease Mentality	Wellness, Potential Model
Fatigues	Regenerates
Self-conscious	Spontaneous
Doubts or believes	Knows
Restricts	Empowers
Takes, Consumes	Gives, Creates
Hesitates	Flows
Moment as means to end	Moment as end in itself

Picture the ego as closing you up, while the spirit opens you up to new resources within yourself—the universe in your mind and heart. Consider just a few of the major changes that occur when you transform yourself from an ego to a spirit mode. Its even more powerful than changing your radio from AM to FM.

1. Transforming myself from self-blaming ego to inspiration spirit produces in me a sensation of not judging myself, but rather inspiring myself.

2. Transforming myself from being threatened by
    outside forces to embracing and incorporating
    those outside forces allows me to absorb and
    grow from an experience, rather than close
    myself off from it because of being threatened.

3. Transforming myself from physical form from
    boundless energy gives me the realization that I
    am more than my body and my physical posses-
    sions. I will live on long after my physical body
    withers away, just as those whose energies have
    touched my life live on in my spirit even after
    their body forms pass. If something can move
    something or someone else, it is proof of its
    existence.

4. Transforming myself from the boundaries of
    this moment in time to a timeless reference
    point allows me to draw resources, strengths
    and insights from a universal time perspective.

5. Transforming myself and my thinking from this
    limited vantage point, this neighborhood place,
    to a new vantage point, the universe, I gain
    resources I was never aware of before. Yet, I can
    do this without leaving my neighborhood. I
    don't have to go somewhere else in the world to
    understand; I only have to go somewhere else in
    my world to understand. The universe is with-
    in.

6. Transforming myself from defending my closed up ego to creating from my opened up spirit expands me to as large as my universal mind.

7. Transforming my ego from a maintenance, protective mode to an enhancement mode enlarges me and grows me to actualize, not just survive.

8. Transforming myself from a disease mentality (what's wrong here?) to a wellness and spiritual, potential model (what is possible here?) changes my focus and the very questions I ask myself in life.

9. Transforming my ego, which gets fatigued under stress, to mobilizing my universal resources to regenerate my energies renews rather than fatigues me.

10. Transforming my self-conscious ego to become universally aware takes the pressure off my efforts and performance. I'm too busy creating out of my spontaneity to notice and judge me.

11. Transforming myself from doubting to knowing gives me the certainty to move forward.

12. Transforming myself from the physical restrictions because of my limited physical ego to empowering myself with deeper powers enlarges my awareness of my already-there universe.

13. Transforming myself from a taking or consuming motivation, to nourish and feed my ego, to a giving and creating motivation enables me to feel my impact on the external world.

14. Transforming myself from a hesitation state to a "flow" mode allows me to get more out of each moment.

15. Transforming myself from using this moment as a means to an end to using it as an end in itself enables me to find rewards now, not wait until later.

LOOK UP OR LOOK DOWN: CHOOSE WHICH WAY YOU WANT TO GO!

Practical intelligence tells us that we see more of whatever we focus on.

We can focus all the things that we don't have. When we choose to look down, we will, immediately begin seeing even more and more of those things we were deprived of. Then we can blame life. And we will start building even a stronger case of how we are persecuted.

Or, we can look up. We can see our abundance. We are alive. We have some love in our lives. Five and one half out of the six billion people in the world would probably change places with us. This is our moment in the history of the magnificent universe. What can we become if we don't look back to who we were?

Which is the intelligent approach to your future: Dwelling on blaming your past, or using your unlimited mind to build your future?

And, which will be more intelligent: To begin tomorrow, or to start today?

See how simple this is becoming? You are getting smarter.

Let's make it last by building your future by making your attitude less dependent upon outside things. That way, we can be fairly sure you are going to keep going.

4

INNER CONFIDENCE

*Lasts Longer Than Outer
Dependency*

Your future is up to one of two things: Either (1) you, or (2) something else outside of you (luck, fate, superstition, the stars, the environment, etc.)

HOW DEPENDENT ARE YOU ON YOUR ENVIRONMENT?

What would you do, if, from this moment onward, for the rest of your life, no one ever again approved of your actions, applauded you, ever told you how great you looked, or ever said, "Good job!"

Would you still survive? Would you start to doubt yourself? Would you go crazy for approval? Would you be weaker and less secure ten years from now?

Or would you start gaining strength from within and keep going forward, driven by your own inner knowing? Would you start realizing that others are probably also so busy being caught up in waiting for approval from others that they didn't have time to approve of you? Wouldn't it be vital and important for you to develop your own inner confidence? Inner confidence is inner security. Your only true security is inside you. Because you will always have you!

THE PERSONAL GROWTH JOURNEY GOING FROM EXTRINSIC TO INTRINSIC MOTIVATION

We are **ex**trinsically motivated when our behavior is determined by external sources, like praise from others or fear of punishment from outside sources. So when our reason for motivation is outside of us, we need to be pushed or pulled, praise and punished from our environment. We give our environment the power. This is when we also, consequently blame our environment for not giving us a pat on the back. When our outside source of motivation is not present, our motivation fades.

When we are extrinsically motivated, we never know how good our day is going to be, because we don't know whether people will be praising us that day.

We are motivated by **in**trinsic factors when we are driven from within. Pride, joy in achievement, the desire for creativity, the feelings of satisfaction of a job well done are all products of intrinsic motivation. Do you remember times when you wanted to achieve something so much, just for the excitement you felt inside you? You, at those times were being pushed by the truest forces of motivation. Yours. This is practical intelligence, because you are with yourself practically all of the time.

When our security foundation is inside us, we are driven by inner forces, and we function just as effectively when we receive reinforcement from without, as when we don't. And when our security is within, we have an internal point of evaluation and can correct and reinforce ourselves.

In his book, *Flow*, Mihaly Csikszentmihalyi records the insights he gained from his study of the healthiest humans. On the subject of inner security verses environmental dependency, he encourages humans to draw from within. This is what the healthiest humans do. Commenting on the paradox that, despite our technological advancement today, we feel more helpless than our ancestors, the author writes,

> *"There is no way out of the predicament than for the individual to take things in hand personally. If values and institutions no longer provide a framework as they once did, each*

*person must use whatever tools are available
to carve out a meaningful, enjoyable life...."*

*"To overcome the anxieties and depressions
of contemporary life, individuals must
become independent of their social environment to the degree that they no longer
respond exclusively in terms of its rewards
and punishments. To achieve such an auton-
omy, a person has to learn to provide rewards
to herself. She has to develop the ability to
find enjoyment and purpose, regardless of
external circumstances."*

The greatest gift that you can give yourself is to trust
yourself, and keep yourself going and going towards your
own self-determined dreams, fueled by your own inner
sources. You always have you.

DEVELOPING INNER SECURITY STARTS
THE PROCESS OF BECOMING A PERSON

In his book *On Becoming a Person*, Carl Rogers describes
the direction a person start to take when moving toward
inner security and intrinsic motivation. Rogers writes,

*" The individual increasingly comes to feel
that the locus of evaluation lies within himself. Less and less does he look to others for
approval or disapproval; for external stan-*

dards to live by for decisions and choices. He recognizes it rests within himself to choose. And the question which matters is, 'Am I living in a way which is deeply satisfying to me, and in a way which truly expresses me.'"

And when you feel alone in the process of becoming your greater self, and the outside world isn't applauding, be aware that you are not alone. All success stories are about people who have taken the journey of inner trust, strength and inner support. Rogers writes:

"El Greco must have realized as he looked at some of his early art work that 'others artists don't paint that way.' But, somehow or other he trusted his own inner experiencing of life, the process of himself, sufficiently that he could go on expressing his own unique perceptions. It was as though he could say, 'Good artists don't paint like this. But I paint like this.'"

"Einstein seems to have been unusually oblivious to the fact that good physicists do not think his kind of thoughts. Rather than drawing back on an inadequate preparation in physics, he simply moved toward being Einstein toward thinking his own thoughts, toward being as truly himself as he could. This is not a phenomenon which occurs only in the artist and genius. Time and again, in

my clients, I have seen simple people become significant and creative in their own spheres, as they developed more trust of the process going on within themselves, and have dared to feel their own feelings, and express them-selves in their own unique way."

Remember the theme of this book, "If it weren't for...., I could be...!" What we blame, we give our power to. Whatever I wait for to keep me motivated, the more I wait. And if the outside source doesn't motivated me, I spend my energies blaming, rather than pulling from within and creating my own path to my self-determined dream. Consider a personal example of the power of inner security, intrinsic motivation and a positive self-image.

ROSE AND CHARLES

One of the most moving experiences I ever had occurred while I was Director of Admissions for an Eastern Pennsylvania college. One day, a 29-year-old women with cerebral palsy arrived at our admissions office door in her wheelchair. Her goal was to attend college. Our interview with her was still in its initial stages when it became obvi-ous that the girl's very serious speech problem made it impossible for a meaningful dialogue to take place. She had to repeat every phrase at least four or five times before we were able to intelligibly connect her utterances. When time and again we failed to understand her words, Rose's head would bend to the side, her face assuming grimaces that reflected her frustration. Patiently she would regroup her energies to try and speak again.

Not only lacking an ability to effectively speak, the young women could barely read, and she could not write at all. She was truly deficient in most of the key skills necessary to achieve success in college. But in spite of all the odds, that "something inside" brought Rose it our admissions office with the goal of becoming a college graduate.

Rose was apparently unaware that the college was unequipped to serve her special needs. Unable to walk without assistance, how could she make it up the steps to the classrooms on the second floor? Lacking the fine coordination to write, how could she take notes? How would she be tested? Which professors would be willing to admit her to their classrooms and face the many burdens and frustrations of dealing with her many special needs? Every thought that could sift though a narrow person's mind seemed to point directly to the conclusion that Rose was not college material and that the college was not prepared to help her climb her ladder of success.

Rose, however, had one asset that helped her soar over all of those mountains of obstacles. The singular but paramount asset was her belief that she could succeed. She had a positive self-image, the key ingredient in the recipe for success. Her self-image and positive attitude that it gave birth to impressed the college admissions staff so much that she was given the green light to attend. After Rose was granted admission to college, a strange thing happened; the college people began to believe in Rose and, in their beliefs, they started to find solutions to deal with each of the barriers, one by one. One administrator even commented that he had seen hundred of students with above average intelligence who did not succeed in college because they lacked what Rose possessed—a positive self-image and a belief that she could succeed. (Allow me to ask you whether you would prefer a brand new automobile in the middle of a desert with no gas in it or an older car with a full tank of fuel. Or would you rather have nothing at all but a tremendous belief and enthusiasm in yourself, or have everything with no hope or self-confidence at all?) Rose had a full tank of enthusiasm, hope, and confidence! She enthusiastically began her college career. Not long after Rose was admitted, I left that college position to work in a private consulting capacity. Consequently, I lost contact with Rose.

The years passed, and I almost forgot about her. However, I was invited to return to that same college to deliver the commencement address for the graduating class of 1980. As I watched the parade of graduates proudly march across the stage at the Rajah Temple in Reading, Pennsylvania, there appeared a little girl wheeling herself across the ceremonial stage. Yes, it was Rose. She knew she could earn her celebrants coming to reap her reward. She knew she could earn her college degree, and she did it. With no high school degree and no ability to write, deficient in her ability to speak, incapable of walking—all of these disability were not powerful enough to keep that "something inside," Rose's positive self-image, from achieving success. As I looked out into the thousands of mostly unknown faces, I saw them unite to stand to show their appreciation to Rose for the gift that she had given to them—a conviction that if you want something in life, to go for it.

The importance of Rose's success story if magnified by the second experience that I had in the same city. Following a motivation workshop that I conducted with the agents of a real estate firm, one of the salespeople came to speak with me. The man, who appeared to be in his early thirties, extended his hand to me and initiated the following dialogue:

"Dr. Losoncy," he inquired, "Do you remember me?"

Apologetically, I responded, "No, I'm sorry."

"I'm Charles_____, I met you about four or five years ago when you were the Director of Admissions at the community college."

"Were you a student there, Charles?"

"No, but at the time I was thinking about attending the college and studying business."

"And you eventually decided not to go?"

"Yeah. You see, more and more I realized that it would probably be too tough. I mean, uh, at the time I had been out of school for about four or five years and had forgotten almost everything I learned in high school. So I decided against going to school at the time. But maybe someday I'll spend some time reading my old high school books and go to college. But I know that if I went now and competed against those kids fresh out of high school, they would snow me."

Rose, the woman with cerebral palsy, who lacked an ability to read, write and speak (but had a lot of inner security), is helping cerebral palsied people. She also inspired a company called Matrix become a leader in producing professional beauty products.

And Charles, the high school graduate who lacked inner security, is unemployed and still looking for a belief in himself. Rose had a disability; she did not have a handicap. Charles did not have a physical disability, but he did have a handicap, He lacked inner security. Who was better off?

The key ingredient for success, the thing inside was Rose life inlook, her inner security. The reason Charles failed was not a lack on intelligence, not limited education, nor bad luck, but rather a lack on inner security.

BUILDING YOUR POSITIVE SELF-IMAGE DEVELOPS YOUR PRACTICAL INTELLIGENCE
(Because a positive self-image works better)

You can change- now. You can make your move towards success at this very moment. You can reach for your dreams by developing yourself, becoming less dependent upon the outside world, and start using your other potential previously hidden. Hidden blaming. You build your inner self by building your own positive self-image.

When your self-image changes, you change your life. Researchers have shown that students have gone from "F" grades to "A" grades in a matter of weeks. Salespeople have literally doubled their income; shy people have become respected leaders; depressed people have developed a renewed enthusiasm for life. All of these changes have occurred because of a change in self-image.

Self-image is the ultimate determiner of personal success or failure. Your self-image is so important that one study after another concludes that your view of yourself is the key factor regulating your life. And the great news is that your self-image can change.

In my search for the answer to the question, "Why do people fail?" I chanced upon a writer who could be considered the first advocate of self-image psychology. In his early insightful book, *Self-consistency: A Theory of Personality*, the educator, Prescott Lecky, argued that people fail, more often than not, not because they are incapable of success. They fail because of their failure self-image. Lecky showed how negative, pre-conceived beliefs and expectations build up resistance and convince people, ahead of time, that it would be impossible for them, with their limited capabilities, to succeed. For example, if a person firmly believes that learning a foreign language would be impossible, the person's self-image will fight, to the bitter end, to keep him or her from achieving success in speaking the new language. The second that the foreign language teacher enters the room, the convinced, "determined" resists the teacher's words.

To disprove the conclusion this person could not possibly learn the new language, note that people tested and labeled retarded have learned foreign languages. But they only learn when they believe they can. If, however, their self-image resists, they will not learn. And, as a more humbling fact, even chimpanzees have learned to understand and respond to the English language. But chimps are lucky. Our hairy friends have an advantage over us. We spend all of our intelligence, reasoning power, and mental energies convincing ourselves that we cannot learn. We conclude that either it would be too difficult to learn, or too humiliating to try and maybe fail. If we used just half of that volcano of misdirected failure energy to actively tackle the task instead, we would move towards success. So fear of failure as a result of a negative self-image is a sure guarantee of failure. With a positive self-image, however, a person envisions success and proceeds ahead to achieve their success.

EXPAND YOUR SELF-IMAGE, EXPAND YOUR PRACTICAL INTELLIGENCE, EXPAND YOUR POSSIBILITIES

Think about your own self-image. Have you ever limited your social possibilities because you believed that there were certain men or women who were out of your social class? If you held these beliefs, what behaviors would your failure beliefs dictate? You probably did not even approach these people to help get the relationship off the ground. Or, if you did approach them, perhaps you said some self-defeating things that sabotaged your chances of developing the relationship. Your self-image actually limited your pool of romantic possibilities. Imagine the number of romantic possibilities you would have, just by expanding your self-image!

Did your self-image tell you that you deserve live in a certain kind of house or that you deserve to have a certain level of income? Did you listen to your self-image and buy that house or work to that exact level of income? And nothing more?

Evidence of the power of self-image is seen everywhere. For example, in the field of organizational development, a common explanation used for decades to demonstrate why promoted people sometimes fail is the well known Peter Principle, theorized by Dr. Lawrence Peter. People who are competent at one level are sometimes promoted to a higher level. The Peter Principle suggests that because the new level demands different skills, they often fail due to the lack of these new skills. The reason they fail, according to the Peter Principle, is because they were promoted to their level of incompetence.

I believe the Peter Principle is only partially correct. I found another reason to explain why some promoted people fail. If someone is promoted to a new position, but his or her self-image views the position as too difficult or overwhelming, this person will fail. With expanding responsibilities, must come expanded self-image. So, people who are promoted, especially those who are promoted quickly, frequently need self-image expansion. Any organization wishing to tap the fuller potential of its people needs to provide some sort of self-image expansion for its family members.

The owner of a major beauty salon in Florida wanted to raise his prices for haircuts, but his hairdressers working for him resisted the price increases. His employees feared that a price raise would result in a loss of customers. I consulted with the owner, advising him that his hairdresser's resistance was not due to their fear of losing customers, but rather their resistance was a result of their low self-image. They saw their styling abilities at too low a level. Their comment that they would lose customers was simply a comment on their self-image. They believed that they were not worth the new service charge. I advised the enthusiastic owner to help the hairdressers to improve their self-images. This would help them to see their worth in new ways. I asked, "Have you asked their hairdressers how much they would pay, not for a haircut, but for courage and confidence and hope? Have you helped them to see their profession, not their jobs, in a new light? If you do, and you help your hairdressers to achieve a more positive and expanded self-image, they will beg for the price increase. The price increase is your comment of respect for them. It shows that you believe in them."

As a former college professor, I would often hear students make dogmatic comments such as, "I'm a B student," or "I'm an average student." I would always think it funny when one of these B students would get an A and share it almost apologetically with me. When I would proudly glance at the student's A grade, I would enthusiastically respond with, "Great job!" Strangely enough, with a self-image lower than the grade the student received, I'd hear something like, "Well, the only reason I received an A was because the professor was easy. I should have earned a B, because I am a B student."

Incredible, isn't it? Have you ever done the same? Why did the student need to apologize for the A?

WHY DO PEOPLE INITIALLY REJECT NEW POSITIVE IDEAS ABOUT THEMSELVES?

Prescott Lecky explained why the self-image, almost always initially rejects a new view of itself. Lecky wrote, "The center or nucleus of the mind is the individual's idea or conception of himself. If a new idea seems consistent with the ideas already present in the system, and particularly with the individual's conception of himself, it is accepted and assimilated easily. If it seems to be inconsistent, it meets with resistance and is likely to be rejected."

Lecky's theory of self-consistency was further supported by researchers who found that peoples' self-images of their abilities were better predictors of how they would achieve than were their IQ's. Imagine that! It is not your abilities, but your beliefs about yourself that hold controlling interest in determining whether you will, or will not succeed. Imagine the devastating cost of a negative self-image, because, in the end, if you believe you are incapable of success, your self-image will work overtime to make sure that success will not happen.

Other researchers concluded from their studies that changes in their self-image lead to changes in achievement.

Again this is powerful and exciting news. Your success is preceded by the belief that you can succeed. If you wanted a few indicators as to well a student would or would not quit school is the student's self-image.

In fact, a key gauge as to how a person will perform in a position is the person's self-image. On these astounding findings, the father of self-image research, William Purvey, writes in relation to school achievement and self-image,

> *"The conclusion seems unavoidable. A student carries with him certain attitudes about himself and his abilities which play the primary role in how well he performs in school."*

Lecky, in fact, wondered why educators gave students remedial training when what they really needed was an altered and positive vision that reflected the belief, "I can and I will learn."

Did you ever see a person labeled "retarded" by one person in the presence of another person who believed in him or her? This performs much more successfully in the presence of the "believer." Consider yourself. Did you ever have a supervisor who didn't believe in you? Everything you did was viewed negatively. What happened? You probably began to feel incompetent. Conversely, did you ever have a supervisor who enthusiastically encouraged you to recognize your strengths and contributions? What happened? You performed—remember, the same you—probably more productively because of the person's beliefs and expectations!

Keep in mind that what you have just read is not opinion—-it is scientifically researched fact. What you see is what you will be!

Concurring with Adler, Lecky, and others, Maxwell Maltz, the world renowned plastic surgeon, wrote on this topic of self-image:

> *The self-image is the key to human personality and human behavior. Change the self-image sets the boundaries of individual accomplishment. It defines what you can and cannot be. Expand the self-image and you expand the area of the possible. The development of an adequately realistic self-image will seem to imbue the individual with new capabilities, new talents, and literally turn failure into success. (Maltz, 1960,p.xix.)*

It is perhaps no news to you that Malt's book, **Psycho-Cybernetics**, is one of the best selling psychological classics of all time. Literally millions of people have been successfully influenced by this "self-determined psychology." Henry Ford's comment, "Believe you can or believe you can't—either way you'll be correct," is in tune with Maltz's and Lecky's and Adler's observations.

HOW DOES SELF-IMAGE
PRODUCE SUCCESS OR FAILURE?

"I could never speak in front of a group"

"I'm not built to be a leader"

"I'm the kind of person who has difficult making decisions"

"Me. I'd never make it in sales. Selling requires something I don't have."

"I'm afraid to try new things and take risks."

"Quit smoking. Not me! I just lack self-discipline."

"No, I'd never ask her out. She'd never want anything to do with someone like me."

"I guess I have about average intelligence."

"I'm the kind of person who is shy."

"I just can't resist snacks."

"I'm not good at opening up new sales accounts."

"I can't take any pressure on the job. I get migraines when given too much responsibility."

"I'm a 'C' student"

"I've gone about as far as I can."

Have you ever heard any statements like these above? Note a few things that each of these statements have in common.

1. Each statement is an echo of an individual's self-image, e.g., "I'm the kind of person who is shy," is a comment on the way the person views him or her self.

2. Each self-image statement is inaccurate, i.e. it can be disprove. As you glance over the list, glance closely at each comment, and you will see that each conclusion could be challenged.

3. Although each self-image statement is inaccurate, the speaker is not consciously aware that each statement is inaccurate, and proceeds through life as if each pronouncement was carved within his or her behavioral granite. The opinion of self is treated by the person as if it were a fact.

4. Each self-image statement limits the individual's potential success. As long as the person believes his or her personal conclusions to be a universal fact, for that exact period of time no growth can occur. These limits are not very practically intelligent.

5. When the individual's subconscious recognizes that the statement is an inaccurate observation which he or she has treated As if it were a fact, he or she then can attack the false conclusion and proceed to expand the self-defeating self-image to

one of success. This process is called self-image modification and is the key way of developing practical intelligence.

Would you agree that a positive self-image works better than a negative self-image?

Using your practical intelligence, you become aware of how a person's negative self-image prevents the individual from going forward and invites the individual to get into a blame mode.

Consider the statement, "I could never speak in front of groups."

This comment is a reflection of the speaker's self-image. The speaker acts as if his or her conclusion is an absolute universal fact.

Ask yourself, "What are facts, and what are opinions?" Two plus two is a fact. Is "I could never speak in front of groups a fact, or an opinion?" Yet the person doesn't know this and treats it as a fact. When the person treats his or her opinion as a fact, this person proceeds based upon the conclusion. These erroneous conclusions direct the person to avoid any situation or opportunity to overcome the "can't." The person's ears quickly perk up to recognize any potentially threatening situation where he or she could possible be asked to speak, and avoids them. So, the person will never experience the chance to disprove the limited conclusion. For the rest of the individual's life, this opinion, treated as fact, will prevent him as achieving success as a public speaker. He needs a change in self-image before success can happen.

The "I could never..." statements are self-defeating. Probably as a toddler the first time you tried to take a step, you felt flat on your face. Suppose you concluded (pre-verbally, of course) that you could *never* walk like mommy and daddy. If you concluded that, you would never try to walk again. After all, you tried to walk one time and you fell flat or your face so you "could never," walk. Imagine the embarrassment you would experience today arriving at a cocktail party...crawling! You would scramble into the room and pull the tablecloth down to reach the hors' de oeuvres!

You succeeded because, when you fell, your self-image kept envisioning yourself as a person who could, or who soon could walk. Fortunately you followed your positive self image that said you could walk, with practice. You did!

Remember the first time you tried to drive a car? You were probably tense, and perhaps your jumpiness caused you to panic and quickly slam on your brakes. Maybe your anxious reaction almost put you and your parents through the front windshield. The earth shattering experience could have even led you to break down in tears, proclaiming dogmatically, "I can never learn to do something as tough as driving a car!"

Maybe you even put yourself down even further because you told yourself that the same task of driving appeared to be so easy for everyone else. A negative self-image steered you away from trying again.

Then something happened. At some point your self-image saw hope and "envisioned" success. Your new capable self-image (practical intelligence at work) may have concluded, "It will be tough to drive, but I will eventually learn how." Maybe you had a few more negative experiences while practicing, but each moment you improved. You soon succeeded.

Now, today with your self-image of, "I am capable," you jump into the car, turn on the ignition, turn on the radio, grab your cell phone, dial a number, and one-handedly drive for miles as you glance at the flashing billboards and scenic mountainsides without a single nervous thought, except for your next car payment!

You achieved success simply as a result of a positive self-image that predicted success. Your positive self-image overcame a few failing incidents by a positive hopeful vision. And you want to make your actions fit your new vision of yourself as a successful driver.

Now reconsider our friend who proclaims, "I could never speak in front of a group." This person is no different than the young child who, "could never walk," or the teenager, who "could never drive." The individual is a diamond with a rough negative self-image, or undeveloped practical intelligence, because this approach isn't working. The culprit denying success for the potential Demosthenes is not a lack of public speaking ability, poor vocabulary, or even fear of groups. The only criminal is the negative self-image that shouts, ""I could never." Think of it. Imagine that this person's self-image instead concluded, "It will be tough, but with some work I could speak in front of groups." What a monumental move to success for the person. Now the blossoming person will develop a new plan of action to overcome these limited visions. A capable and positive self-image is the key ingredient to start the success snowball rolling.

OVERCOMING SELF-IMAGE PROBLEMS: BEEN THERE, DONE THAT!

I chose the example of public speaking because it touches home with me. I would like to share with you a personal story.

A few decades ago, I went to hear a lecture. While watching the dynamic speaker, I became inspired that what he did was what I was going to do someday. I became determined to be the best speaker I could be in my lifetime. However, I wasn't talented in speaking. In fact, my vocabulary and grammar scores could win almost any limbo contest. I was frightened to death about even the thought of speaking in front crowds of people. So I had a lot, a whole lot to overcome.

However the only resistance I had to overcome was in my mind. I visualized success and I wanted it. I knew there was absolutely no way I wouldn't reach my goal. After all, I had a lifetime.

Because I visualized my goal and became determined, my course was locked in. My compass was pointed towards a goal. My self-image believed that, "With much work, it could be accomplished." So I developed my plan. My ears and eyes were wide open to sense opportunities to observe good speakers. I traveled great distances just to watch speakers' professionals mannerisms, demeanor, expressions, words, topic titles. Keep in mind that I would have never done this if my self-image had concluded, a head of time, that my goal was unattainable.

I started my first lectures by talking with chairs in my living room, imagining these chairs were real people. Fortunately, there were very few questions following these speeches. I looked into a mirror when I spoke and developed expressive looks and hand gestures. I followed this by taking every opportunity I had to speak to small groups. I walked to improve my vocabulary and grammar. I literally did everything consistent with meeting my goal.

I had many, many setbacks, and still do today, three decades later. Its tough watching people yawn, roll their eyeballs or leave in the middle of a speech. But remembering my goal, I told myself that these experiences were a necessary part of the journey to reach my destination.

As I think about it today, the destination was inevitable since I visualized my goal and concluded that there was no way I couldn't reach it. When discouraged, my self-image kept envisioning a sign on the highway of life which read:

Next Exit — Nowhere
Straight Ahead — Everywhere

I'm still on that road following my compass that points to success, Today, I make my living through speaking. That tells me that every single time I told myself, "I could never speak in public," I was wrong. I always could. I just needed a self-image that concluded, ahead of time that the day would come when I would reach my goal. Once I prophesied success, I developed my plan and moved towards my goal. If I made a mistake, I simply corrected the problem, The next time I moved closer to my goal.

On this highway of life, successful achievement of your goals is like driving your car from New York to Los Angeles. When you start, you are at the farthest point from your goal. You cannot possibly be at your goal the moment you start, but you keep focusing of the fact that you are moving towards your goal. Your practical intelligence reminds you that you are getting closer and closer. That view works. If you keep your goal firmly in mind, when your car breaks down, you simply fix it, and get on your way. Complaining about the disabled car only wastes your valuable success time and delays your victory celebration.

SELF-IMAGE PROPHESIES
SUCCESS OR FAILURE

David's job interview is only a few minutes away. As the 20 year-old waits tensely outside the personnel manager's office, he thinks about how unsuccessful he had been in previous interviews. Reflecting on the last four jobs he didn't get, he thinks, "Why should this one be any different?' In addition to being on a job seeking losing streak, he reminds himself about all of the news on how tight the job market is. In addition he is certain that there are many, many people much more qualified for this job than he is. Although his background fits the requirements on paper, he thinks there surely will be someone else who has either more experience, more education or more of an, "in." He slumps in his chair as he looks around the room crowded with competition, he is sure, for the same job. And he is sure that everyone one of them has something that he lacks. To escape eye-to-eye contact with his competitors, he glances at the secretary. She appears to be meticulously organized and aloof. She peers at David over the top of her glasses and gives an intimidating look. David squirms again. His heart is pounding, his voice seems to be leaving him, his palms are sweating, his chin is quivering, and his knees are shaking. He wants to leave and, at that moment, the personnel manager opens the door, and announces his name, requesting that he come into the office to begin the interview.

Jonathan's job interview is only a few minutes away. This 20 year-old man waits outside the personnel manager's office with eager anticipation. He begins to think about how he can be a success on the job once he gets the position. He analyzes the position he is seeking and lives a day in the life of that person in that capacity. It is a position in which he would be dealing with people. Jonathan then imagines that he owns the company. He wonders what kind of a person he would want in that position for his company. What kind of attitudes would he be looking for in the people he would hire? He concludes that he would want a person who likes people, who is confident, is open for new ideas, is enthusiastic, and who would make a good company employee. Yes, Jonathan thinks, to be a good company employee it would be wise to learn even more about the company. He looks around the reception area and finds a company brochure on the table. He pages through the brochure and becomes increasingly excited about the company. He learns some interesting facts about the size and scope of the operation. This news excites him and tells him of the opportunities to grow. Jonathan looks at the many offices and imagines himself with an office of his own someday soon. The secretary, obviously efficient, stares over her glasses at him, and Jonathan gives her a big ear to ear smile.. She smiles back. Jonathan feels great inside and thinks how warm the people are here at this company. He is also impressed with her efficiency and kindly shares with her his observation.

Impressed, he comments, "I really admire your organization. Are you one of those naturally organized people?" The secretary replies, "I guess I enjoy my work." She smiles again. He already feels he belongs there. And he does. And he soon will be.

The door opens and the personnel manager invites Jonathan into his office.

David and Jonathan are stories of life. David's negative self-image dictated to his whole viscera the notion that he doesn't deserve the position, and that he will never get it. as a result David's self-image worked vigorously to defeat him. The personnel manager, in reading David's confidence level, saw him as a person who would be too timid, too defensive to be part of a growing, assertive company. David does not get the position and he is defeated again. For the next job interview, his self-image will be even more negative. The lad's self-image predicted failure and the prediction was accurate. Low practical intelligence develops a view of life that doesn't work.

Jonathan, on the converse, carries a self-image that announces the arrival of success. Jonathan predicted success for himself and thus used his energies to make that success happen. While David squirmed in his seat, Jonathan went ahead to learn more about the company, imagining what kind of employee the company needed in that position, and, in fact, ignited his own enthusiasm for the job.

The same situation was faced by David and Jonathan. David and Jonathan's college grades were the same. Yet observe how different the situation looked to each because of different self-images. David saw obstacles, Jonathan saw opportunities.

If you were the personnel manager, who would you hire?

Your self-image produces success or failure by prophesizing or subconsciously predicting success or failure before it happens. And self-image, more often than not, is accurate. Practical intelligence tells us that moving ahead with certainty gives you the winner's edge.

In this chapter we further developed our practical intelligence by becoming intrinsically motivated, driven from within. With our security inside of ourselves, we no longer need to lean on the world for reinforcement and support. It is inside us.

Now, let's improve our practical intelligence by finding ways of humorously accepting and loving tough realities in the world.

> *"If it weren't for all the things that shouldn't be (according to me), I could be happy!"*

5

ACCEPTANCE

*Frees Us Faster
Than Blaming Reality*

LOVE WHAT YOU CAN'T CHANGE. WHY? BECAUSE YOU DON'T HAVE TO DWELL ON IT ANYMORE

I love the weather. I was going to be a meteorologist until I found out there was some math involved. And, on top of that, science. All of us discipline problems were pretty good at math because whenever we acted up in grade school, the nun would give us math drill cards to do after school. And it seemed to me that after doing the late weather after 11, I didn't want to hang around dividing seven digit numbers by four digit numbers.

Anyway, I love the weather, and my favorite station is the weather channel. Why? Because it is a place I can relax. I do not have the tension like I do watching Regis ask questions and not getting them right, or running out of lifelines. I do not play a role in the weather. I can watch it unfold, unlike a TV program or a movie, where people are just getting paid to mimic the words of a writer, weather is real. I love the weather because the pressure is off me.

I can't change the weather. I love things I can't change. I can take my energies somewhere else. That's where the pressure is on.

REALITY HAS MORE IMPORTANT THINGS TO DO THAN TO PUT CHALLENGES IN MY WAY

When the light turns red, it means stop. Nothing more, nothing less. Some people give that light more power than it has. Perhaps you have even seen people talk to traffic lights, even yell at them. I suspect that the light is unaffected by this useless monologue.

But some of my friends who are unbendingly determined to make themselves miserable at every opportunity, caution me that if you yell at the light long enough, and loud enough, it will soon change. They are right. The light will change in about 30–45 seconds, either way!

When we find ourself on what seems to be a bumpy road and realize that is a flat tire instead, the person with practical intelligence decides that a great choice would be to pull over and fix the flat tire. Nothing more, nothing less. The person, a little slower to grab hold of what is happening here, immediately goes into the blame mode, searching mentally for people and things to blame.

"These tires are no good."

"This car always has a problem."

"If my boss gave me that pay raise I deserve, I could have bought better tires."

"These roads are rotten."

"My wife forgot to send in my AAA's renewal card. I'll have to pay to have this thing towed."

"Why didn't I put a spare in the car after the last flat?"

This blaming, of course, could go on forever. The amount of things we blame for our situation is only limited to our creative mind's determination to avoid taking action and solving the problem. Remember, these events are neither good nor bad. They just are!

The person with practical intelligence wants to make the connection between cause and effect, and then solve the problem.

"Hmm, the car is wobbling, but the road looks fine. It must be a flat tire. Thank God, I understand what the problem is. I'll pull over to the side and fix it. I will have the car towed since I don't have a spare."

Notice, stress free by solving instead of blaming.

Love the things you can't change. Why? Because you don't have to worry about them. You can't change them anyway. And then focus your energies on the things you can change.

I FOUGHT REALITY & REALITY WON

I believe that life is incredibly simple and that is people who make it complex. Most people frustrate themselves and make their lives difficult by making THE ULTIMATE HUMAN EXPERIENCE—the mistake of losing sight of reality. 99% of us are partially out of touch with reality at one time or another. These are the times when we confuse "what we wish to be" with "what actually is" in life. We reduce ourselves to having the intelligence of a dog chasing the wheels of a car. Instead, succeed by saving yourself a lot of energy by chiseling these three words into your mental fabric: "What Is, Is."

Motivation lectures and positive attitude books often neglect an important point about reality. Your start toward Success City is reality. If you are so high that you think you could fly, it would be a grave error to ignore the reality of the law of gravity. As Bertrand Russell once commented, "Any man who maintains that happiness comes wholly from within should be prepared to spend thirty-six hours in rags in a blizzard without food." This point is not meant to discourage you. I feel, perhaps, a parental need not to have you fall flat on your face. That will only discourage you and keep you from being successful, thus not helping the rest of humanity. We need you. So face the fact that there will be barriers, but through creative thinking, enthusiasm, and goal setting, these obstacles can be overcome. So when I say, "What Is, Is," it is meant to encourage you. When you accept this fact of reality, you have an invigorating, challenging starting point. Dreamers who faced reality and learned how to reach the heavens despite the realities of gravity were those who designed planes and spacecraft. Wishers, on the other hand, who didn't take reality into consideration only experienced frustration. Increase you Practical Intelligence by getting a keen sense of reality. Never again be frustrated by putting reality "where it isn't."

SEEING REALITY FOR WHAT IT IS

Lock into your mind forever these three facts about reality, and you will find yourself managing your life by a realistic goal orientation:

FACT 1: Reality is not what we wish it to be; rather, reality is what it is.

FACT 2: Reality is not interested in what each of us thinks it "should be," rather, reality is what it is.

FACT3: Reality is not just or fair; rather, reality is what it is.

FACT

1

Reality is not what we wish it to be; rather, reality is what it is.

Don't get caught in the "wisher's web." Reality has no respect for wishers. Wishing away a thunderstorm or wishing a million-dollar-lottery win are in the almost guaranteed routes of failures. Not only is wishing an ineffective course of action, but it is a frustrating route as well. That is what concerns me about you. I don't want you to be discouraged in your trip to Success City because you made the error of wishing that the 200-mile journey was only 50 miles and eventually became frustrated. It is 200 miles. But after facing reality head on, if you use creative thinking and enthusiasm, you will find a way. People living in the Sea of Fantasy off of the Coast of Reality dream up a world that doesn't exist, and then they get frustrated when the world they wished for "lets them down." The world, in fact, didn't let them down. The problem was that they were living on wishes which were false "pick-me-up" in the first place. If you want to eat, stop wishing and start fishing. Don't compromise one moment of your dream; just make sure that you are clear that your starting point is on firm ground.

FACT

2

Reality is not interested in what each of us thinks it "should be;" rather, reality is what it is.

Most of the people in the world bat their heads up against the wall of reality by confusing what they think "should be" with what actually is. If you take the following sentence and make it part of your life, you will never again be unhappy or frustrated for more than just a few seconds. Here it is: THERE ARE NO SHOULDS, OUGHTS, OR MUSTS IN THE WHOLE WORLD... NONE! EVERY TIME WE SAY ANY OF THOSE WORDS, WE ARE RUNNING FULL FORCE AWAY FROM REALITY. INSTEAD OF SAYING "SHOULD," "OUGHT," OR "MUST," LEARN THE ONLY WORDS THAT WILL LEAD TO SUCCESS. What are those magic words? They are: WHAT IS MY PLAN? Observe how people sit in their SHOULD seats and run away from reality. Allow me to share a few of my experiences with SHOULD THINKERS.

A client of mine who came late for one of our appointments told me apologetically, "I'm sorry I'm late, but I caught ten red lights in a row. You should never get that many." My response was the only logical one I could give. I asked Barb, "Exactly how many red lights SHOULD you get? Think about it.

While speaking at a teachers' convention in Edmonton, Alberta, one of the bellhops at the hotel apologized to me for the freezing weather. The kind man said, "I responded again in the only logical way I knew. I asked, "How cold SHOULD it be? He had, believe it or not, an answer. He knocked my socks off by responding, "It should be about ten degrees warmer." Although I was taken back by his response, I was taken back by his response, I wasn't finished comment that " it SHOULD be about ten degrees warmer." I asked, "WHATS YOUR PLAN?"

A fellow professor with whom I shared an office was angrily hovering over his desk one day demanding, "I left my car keys on the desk. They SHOULD be there! Looking at the empty desk, I retorted, "But they're not." While pointing accusingly to his desk, he came back with, "But they SHOULD be." "But they're not," I said again. "But they SHOULD be," he growled. I informed the professor that he at least two options. I said, " It seems to me that the keys, whether they SHOULD or SHOULD be on your desk, are, in fact, not on your desk. Believe me, there is a greater chance that your keys are in Rio than there is of them being here on the desk. There are at least one or two things you could do. You could, for the rest of your life, stand by this desk and say, " The keys SHOULD be here," or secondly, you SHOULD here,' or secondly, you could look elsewhere. Which decision would help you to find your keys?

Another friend of mine, who was usually quite in touch with reality, had one weak moment. Quiet annoyed, Carol said to me, "My oil burner broke down and it SHOULDN'T. It was just checked, and I even have a warranty."

I asked, "Did you show the oil burner the warranty? "I went on to add, "For the rest of your life, you can stand by the oil burner, chanting, 'You SHOULD work, you SHOULD work, because I have a warranty,' or you call to get it fixed. Take just a few minutes to think the matter through.

Which do you think would be a more productive course of action?

Finally, I won't leave this topic on reality until I relate this incredible experience. At a party, I listened to someone say that she began her diet. I was elated for her goal-setting spirit. Soon afterward, we arrived at a birthday party. It wasn't long before the hostess was walking with her tray, serving cake and ice cream. When the bright-eyed women turned to us, she enticed my friend, who had just claimed she started her diet that day, by asking, "Would you care for some marble cake and ice cream?"

Hold on to your sombrero when you hear, in this chapter on reality, my friend's response.

"Oh, I SHOULDN'T have any cake...but I guess it won't hurt!

I looked at her and responded, "What would be your second guess?"

Yes, LIFE IS INCREDIBLY SIMPLE, but people make it difficult when they do as psychologist Albert Ellis says, "They SHOULD on themselves."

Eliminate the words "should, "ought", and "must" and instead say, "WHAT IS MY PLAN?" You will be amazed how many people fail have vocabularies filled with those unproductive words. Become a "WHATS-MY-PLAN?" thinker.

FACT

3

Reality is not just or fair; rather, reality is what it is.

It would do my mind and heart a lot of good if I didn't have to write this because it is inconsistent with my former strongly held beliefs. But it appears to me that if you want to succeed and help the world, you need to accept the fact that REALITY IS NEITHER JUST NOR FAIR. The minute that we allow this insight to permeate our minds, that's the minute that we can bring about a positive change. Observe Kathy, who's caught in the unfairness trap:

> Kathy: It just isn't fair. Carolyn can eat all of the pastry that she wants, and she never gains a pound. Yet, if I so much as look at cakes or cookies, I put on weight.

Where does Kathy take her complaint? Right, there is nowhere to go! Kathy is producing her own frustration because she believes that reality is not fair to her. Her frustration, remember, is not due to the fact she gains weight, but is related to her unwillingness to accept reality the way it "is." Imagine if Kathy accepted the fact that she gains weight easily and used all of her energies to plan a diet, instead of using her energies to complain. We ask Kathy is destined to a life of frustration because she does not accept an element of the world that she believes does not work in her favor.

We might mention to Kathy, "Yes, it is unfair. But maybe, if you think of it, the unfairness of life has actually worked in your favor. For example, you have a healthy heart, you eat three meals as day, you have the ability to read, you have two TV's, and most of the people in the world would enthusiastically change places with you at this moment today. Yes, true, the world is unfair, but look to what you have and develop a plan to help other people."

It is important for me to say here that justice is a most noteworthy ideal and that I would be glad to be right up front leading the parade for a more just world. But the fact is that the world is not just or fair, and demanding that it be so is not only ineffective, but frustrating. Together, let's develop a plan to change that fact. Together, let's develop a plan to change that fact.

JUST BECAUSE YOU CAN'T DO EVERYTHING DOESN'T MEAN YOU CAN'T DO ANYTHING

Once a person who has developed his practical intelligence meets reality head on, face to face, and decides that he would rather accept what he chooses not to change that fight the uphill battle, his energies are freed to face the challenges on the ground.

I can't live forever. I can't fly without help.
But I can:

1. choose my attitude

2. compliment a friend

3. smile

4. exercise and feel great after

5. dress up

6. choose what I will eat tonight

7. write a poem

8. decide between a mounds bar and an almond joy
   next time I am in a store

9. think of people who love me

10. go to the public library

11. say, "I'm sorry"

12. give a hug

13. make a child's day

14. create

15. listen

16. sing

17. write a poem

18. forgive

19. take a walk

20. take a hot bath

21. jump rope

22. climb a small tree

23. listen to my favorite music

24. have dinner tonight, with candle light

25. buy someone a card

26. make a card for someone

27. try to make my own soft pretzels

28. go to a movie

29. thank someone for doing something very ordinary

30. see the people around me in new, fresh, exciting ways

31. leave a note at home for my loved ones to discover

32. remember how much I wanted my spouse a few years back

33. go to a public park

34. bounce a ball

35. include somebody who feels left out

36. set new goals

37. borrow a dog

38. read a positive book

39. write a letter to the president and see if I get one back

40. try to do a pushup

41. enroll in a karate class and see if I can get to the second belt

42. realize how great a really good apple or pear can taste

43. imagine anything

44. mix ice cream flavors together to create a new one

45. try to guess how fast elephants can run

46. conduct a survey with people on a topic I am interested in

47. read the **Guinness Book of Records** and see which one I have the best chance of beating

48. take the coke pepsi test and see how accurate I am

49. go to a flower shop

50. estimate the amount of steps it takes me to walk the block in front on my house

Just because you can't live forever or fly by yourself today doesn't mean you can't do anything.

WHEN SOMEONE SAYS, "FACE REALITY," THANK THEM!

A friend of mine was listening to my wild idea, and stopped me with a, "face reality." He was focusing in on all of the barriers I would face in attempting to get this idea off the ground. At first, his comment stopped my momentum. I started reflecting on the challenges, the problems, the probability and found myself creating my own discouragement. I was subconsciously blaming reality. It shouldn't be this difficult.

Then I listened to his words, "Face Reality," a different way. If I am going to face reality, the starting point of reality is that, "I am alive. And that wouldn't have to be!"

I turned to my friend who just cautioned me to face reality and shook his hand, before the ran up the street inspired.

I exclaimed, "Thank you so much Bob. Occasionally I do forget to face reality. Occasionally I don forget that I am alive, am lucky enough to have a great wife and daughter, to have a good job, to live in America and to be in good health, three meals a day, a home, a car. Thank you.

Sometimes we hear, "Face reality," the wrong way. The way that doesn't work. Develop your practical intelligence and face reality. And thank others when they remind you to do, as well.

YOU ARE TRYING WAY TOO HARD

After arriving in Dallas to speak at a convention, someone stops me in the hallway and says, "I didn't know you were going to be here at the convention. I am so excited to meet you. I am going to try to get into your talk tomorrow morning."

I grabbed my heart, looked all fatigued, weak and drained-out, and responded, "Oh no, please, please don't try. I'm already burnt out thinking about how hard you are going to have to work at this trying. In fact, you now have to do two thing to get to the talk; first, you have to try. Then, second, you are going to have to get there. This is overwhelming, my hearts beating fast, I'm sweating, I'm close to having an anxiety attack. Everytime I have to try, it usually is so overwhelming and draining, I can't get it done."

I stopped for a moment to observe his confused face and added, "My friend. Don't make it so hard on yourself. Stop trying, and instead just show up over there in the Enterprise Room at eight am. But if you have to try, you'll never make it."

As I arrived at seven am the next morning in the room, there was my newfound friend already seated. The first one in the classroom.

"I see you didn't try to get here today, huh? I asked.

"No way. This was too important for me to try to be here. I just decided to be here. It was effortless," he responded.

When you ask your daughter to clean up her room, and she tells you she'll try, let her know that you are not asking that much out of her.

"Oh honey, I'm not asking for you to go that far and try. I'm not asking that you do two things, first to try and then, to actually do. I'm just asking that you take action and clean up your room. It'll be so much easier if you don't have to try first."

After a confused silence, you'll start to hear the vacuum cleaner on. You've taken away the hard work of trying so that she can effortlessly go about the business of cleaning up her room.

WATCH YOUR LANGUAGE

We don't know reality directly; we know it through the words we choose to use. Words are powerful, emotional triggers.

In **What is, is!**, Diane Losoncy and I suggested words to eliminate from our vocabulary to develop our practical intelligence.

Eliminate, "shoulds," "oughts," and "musts." We learned these from our teacher, Albert Ellis. As I discussed earlier in this chapter, reality is not the way we want it to be; reality is the way it is. Some people get angry and blame the world for it not being the way they want it to be. They then demand that the universe adjust itself to be more convenient for them. You can see their demands in the frequent uses of their words, "should," "ought," and "must."

Consider the grandiosity inherent in these statements:

"The weather shouldn't be this cold in June"

"I went over to Europe to visit. I was only there a few days and came home. There are too many foreigners there. There oughta be more Americans"

"My car must not run out of gas just because its empty"

Curiously there is not a single should, ought or must in the real world. We create our own ideal (ideal for me) world every time we use one of these words. Plus, we run away from the real world of, "What is, is!" We produce our own frustration when we demand that the world be better for me than it is.

As we eliminate the shoulds, oughts, and musts, let's find more rational words to take the sting out of our psychic pain.

Language Problem	Language Revealing Practical Intelligence
"It shouldn't be this cold"	"I would prefer that it was warmer, but it is 2 degrees. I'll bundle up"
"There oughta be more	"I personally would feel more comfortable Americans" if there were more Americans in Europe, but what is, is"
"My car must not run out of gas"	"It would be more convenient for me if my car made it to a gas station, but when there is more gas in the car, then it is what is called, "out of gas." It needs gas and will stop without it. This not a personal event because anybody, whose car is out of gas, would also have a car that would stop."

DEVASTATED OR INCONVENIENCED?

Since events become whatever we label them, we play a role in how much an event impacts us by the words we choose to give to the event.

While speaking about turning catastrophes into incon-veniences in Des Moines, Iowa to a group of about 1500 hairdressers, I tripped over my microphone wire. I fell off the stage and landed on the floor. The group of mid-west-erners were polite and concerned. As I picked myself up and walked back on to the stage, I reacted, "That, for example was an inconvenience."

The silence was broken as the group started to chuckle.

"Yes," I ad-libbed, "that was an inconvenience. Why? Because I fell and I hurt myself a little. Was it a tragedy? No. Could it have been? Yes, of course, if I called it a 'tragedy.' If I labeled the event a 'tragedy,' I probably would have not walked back on to the stage. I also may have quit speaking for a living. Or I could make it an catastrophe by calling it a catastrophe. But I choose to call it an inconvenience. So that is what it becomes to me. "

I continued, "Now, to be honest with you, did I want to fall? Well, if it was on a ballot, I would have voted, 'no.' But should I have fallen? Of course, because the only thing underneath my feet was air. I had to have fallen!"

Years later, a lady in that group moved to Wyoming. One evening, she drove her car into her beauty salon. Her hus-band was in the car with her. Can you imagine. There is she in her car, in her beauty salon in a state of panic. And all of a sudden, remembering the program in Iowa, she started to laugh and cry at the same time and turned to her husband and said, "This is just an inconvenience." They backed their car out, they hugged, and they planned their new salon.

Years later she told me, "Dr. Lew, you have to come see our new salon. Its beautiful. And, you know, fortunately we'd been through a minor inconvenience. Had we been through a tragedy, we could have never bounced back. But if go through a minor inconvenience, like we did, it doesn't take long to rebuild."

Watch your language. Don't make a tough reality tougher. You get tougher, and the tough reality melts in your will.

THANK YOUR CRITICS FOR THE FREE ADVICE

Part of dealing with reality is handling criticism from others. The person who needs practical intelligence development, when criticized;

- gets hurt

- attacks the critic ("You're not so hot yourself")

- defends ("If it weren't for...")

- denies

- most unfortunately, misses information

Contrarily, the person with high practical intelligence welcomes criticism as a source of potential learnings. When criticized, he listens to the criticism and simply asks himself the question, "How can I use the information he is giving me to help me become a better person?"

You'll notice, there is no pain, hurt, anger or desire for revenge, and no defensiveness. Just a simple determination to learn and to grow.

Think of the last time someone criticized you. Block out everything but the person's words and your desire to focus in on how you can use the person's words to become the best you can be. Let it in.

Make a mental note of what you learned.

Now respond defensively and personally to the critic's attack, and see what you learn and how you feel.

You probably sense that when you handled the criticism with practical intelligence and a desire to learn and grow, you didn't get upset or hurt, didn't experience anger or a desire for revenge, didn't think of the critic's imperfections, and, most importantly, you got information that can help you to grow.

Maybe you even have a desire to thank the critic. All of those benefits come to you by making a choice to accept reality, instead of blaming it. That's why that decision is called practical intelligence. Because it works much, much better.

Instead of blaming reality, we developed our practical intelligence to not only accept, but to love things we choose not to change. Now let's find ways of encouraging people in our home or workplace rather than blaming them.

6

ENCOURAGING OTHERS

*Gets Better Results
Than Blaming Them*

A PERSONAL EXPERIENCE
ON THE POWER OF ENCOURAGEMENT

I graduated 309 out of 321 at Reading Central Catholic High school in Pennsylvania. This actually appears better than it really was since I had some teachers who gave me the benefit of the doubt, in the last minute finding a way to turn that F into the D. I keep telling myself that their motivation was not just to move me on, and not be in their class the following year.

In my junior year, while at one point I was failing five out my six subjects, the cigar smoking principal asked me to justify.

"How do you explain this, Lewis? Five F's and a D!"

"I'm just putting too much time in that subject I'm getting a D in," I analyzed."

Fr. Leichner didn't seem to understand.

The same year, the English teacher suggested that I may have been copying from another student.

"Lewis, you had ninety-nine right out of a hundred."

"Thank you sister."

"Lewis, I noticed that you sat right beside David. And David is our top student."

"I don't remember where I sat that day."

"Well, interestingly, David, our top student, also, like you, Lewis, also had ninety-nine right out of a hundred."

"Wow, I'm in good company, sister."

"And even more interesting Lewis, is that both you and David missed the same question, number 56."

"He and I must think alike, sister."

"Or is it possible that you were copying from David, Lewis?"

I sensed where she was going with this. And I knew I could help her with her concerns. I had this bright idea.

"Sister, how about if we look at both papers, David and mine. If we both wrote the same answer for number 56, the one we both had wrong, that would certainly prove one of us had copied. But, if we had two different answers for number 56, than that is proof that neither David, nor I were copying. Do you agree? Doesn't that make sense?"

"I guess it does," she hesitatingly responded.

She got both papers out, and I proved to here that I could not have been copying because, fortunately for both of us, we had two different answers for number 56. I'll never forget it.

David wrote, "I don't know."

And I wrote, "Neither do I."

It was there, that day, that I found out that two people looking at the same thing could see two different things in it.

But, back to the encouragement. One day, while walking down the school halls, our guidance counselor, who was also a priest, stopped me, looked me in the eyes, and smiled.

"You are fantastic!"

I never recalled a dialogue like this before. I wondered what his angle was.

"Could you tell me just a little bit more father?"

"Yes, I saw two nuns walking down the hallways, and you had them so upset I think the one was almost swearing."

"Is that good?"

"Well, it sure shows you have a talent."

"What's that?"

"Well if you can make nun's swear, it shows that you have the ability to influence people. Did you ever think about how you could use that talent?"

"I never knew I had it, until now."

"Well someday, you could become a teacher, or a salesman."

Somebody saw something positive in me. That night I went home and I did something rare. I studied. And the next day I got a B+ in a geometry test. Who did I take my grade to? Of course, my encourager. And the good priest looked me in the eyes again, and suggested that I can focus on my weaknesses or I can focus on my strengths. He asked me which approach I thought would work better.

My encourager changed my life by helping me see what was right with me. I was so accustomed to hearing about my deficiencies and what was wrong, that I thought my weaknesses defined me. I learned that a person has both positives and negatives, and that successful people choose to focus on the positives.

Like the positive priest, we can choose to see what is right with people. I believe that the priest, and our own experiences, would tell us this approach works better than blaming people and centering on their weaknesses.

In the workplace, we can blame people for being lazy or we can develop approaches to encourage them.

ON ENCOURAGEMENT IN THE WORKPLACE, SURVEY SAYS...

It becomes clear, after a while in life that blaming another person for being lazy doesn't exactly move them, except to defend, makes excuses, fight back, blame us, etc., etc. And then the vicious cycle gets worse, and we find ourselves way off the issue. In my book, *The Motivating Team Leader*, I listed the qualities that people, in a survey, responded with were present in their most discouraging and most encouraging leaders. The responses were so significant because there were so many areas of agreement.

First, to the question relating to the qualities of the most discouraging leader:

1. Always pointed out what I was doing wrong. Never what I was doing right.

2. Never listened to me

3. Had double standards, one for his favorites, another for the others.

4. Know it all

5. Stole your ideas

6. No time for you

7. Didn't trust you

8. Talked down at you

9. Gave you false hopes

10. Belittled you

11. Made you feel like an underdog

12. Took advantage of you

13. Gave you only negative feedback

14. Set up inconsistent rules

15. Lied

16. Would fly off the handle. You would live in fear when he was around.

17. Took on all of your responsibilities. You felt like you were totally unimportant.

18. Used her position to overpower me

19. Gave no direction. I didn't even know what doing a good job meant.

20. Would say things like, "I'll see you in my office after work." And that was the first thing in the morning.

21. Intimidated and stressed you.

22. Would put your ideas down

23. Keeps laying on you extra things to do without ever even saying, "Thanks"

24. Negative attitude

25. Saw you as important only as someone who produced. Never noticed that you were a person.

26. Constantly compared you to other people.

27. Made you feel unwanted. Like at staff meetings, never even looked at you.

28. Smooth talker, but no substance.

29. Never satisfied, nit picker

30. Would show you how much he produced, when he was in your job, before you.

31. Always had to get the last word in.

32. Would make you take his responsibilities, like dealing with tough, angry customers.

33. Would yell at you in front of others. I felt so small.

34. Played favorites.

35. Would socialize with the men and not the women. It gave the men the edge for promotion.

36. Critical facial expressions. I remember especially the heavy eyebrows.

37. You'd bat your brains out working and it was never noticed.

38. Used sarcasm and embarrassment.

39. Assumed I knew what he wanted or what he was thinking.

40. Closed-minded

Now, here is a list of the responses to the most encouraging leader:

1. Listened to you, he really listened.

2. Believed in me, even more than I believed in myself.

3. He noticed what you did right, as well as pointing areas where you can develop yourself

4. Could delegate responsibility

5. Enthusiasm

6. Sense of humor

7. Admitted mistakes himself

8. Gave you credit for your ideas.

9. Could recognize when you needed a lift and was there.

10. Interested in you as a person.

11. Was at peace with himself

12. Consistent

13. Good teacher, willing to share ideas

14. Criticized constructively

15. Followed through on promises

16. Honest, genuine, real

17. Positive

18. Permitted freedom and independence as long as you got the job done. You didn't feel smothered or claustrophobic

19. Gave you a feeling that things you said in confidence would be left in confidence.

20. Said, "Hello," or "Glad to see you," in the morning.

21. I'd hear comments from my manager's boss to me like, "Bob tells me what a great job you are doing." That would really give me a lift.

22. Accepted me even if I pointed out how things could be better in the department or if I criticized him.

23. She showed how what you did for the company was important.

24. Helped me feel like part of the team.

25. Did little things like reassure me after I came back from vacation that I was missed.

26. I knew exactly what was expected of me.

27. I felt very creative around him. Even if he didn't like my idea, he would still appreciate my efforts.

28. My first day on the job he took me around to meet everybody. I felt immediately accepted.

29. Fair but firm

30. Vulnerable. Would share his own shortcomings.

31. He would always be available to talk to. Gave you time.

32. Believed in me. I felt special and unique. And so did everybody.

33. Would remember our conversations.

34. Open-minded.

35. Non-defensive.

36. Gave good leadership. Could lift the team's spirits. Saw obstacles as challenges.

37. Was a terrific example. I even quit smoking and started dieting after her example. She was a total person.

38. Professional—never backbiting or putting people down. Even when he was attacked he listened and rationally explained his position.

39. Warm, but not a warmth stemming from weakness

40. After disciplining you, he gave you hope and a new start.

11 ENCOURAGING APPROACHES TO SPARK PEOPLE UP

1 **Make each person you meet significant.** Meet people in a special way. In a world in which every one is a number most places that they go, quickly recognize the person inside the worker, the clerk, the custodian or whatever they do. Treat them like the unique person they are. Genuinely care and spend more than 50% of your conversation time talking about them and their interests and concerns. Use his or here name frequently and make it a point to remember special details.

2   **Focus on strengths and potential.** Condition yourself to focus in on what's right with people rather than dwelling on what's wrong. We all know people who are nit pickers and flaw finders and are experts on seeing what is wrong. Be an individual who is finely tuned to see what's right in the other person.

Develop your strength focusing skills by conditioning yourself to immediately zero in on the assets and potential in the people you meet.

Be a "pick-em-up," type of person with every one you meet. You've heard the expression, "Here comes bad news!" Be a good news giver so that when people see you, your very presence gives them a lift.

Develop the talent to see assets even in peoples' liabilities and weaknesses. Remember what the encouraging guidance counselor did for me. He saw my strengths under my weaknesses.

3   **Be quick to recognize progress and improvement.** Your child is so excited. The three year old puts on her own shoes for the first time. they are on backwards. She can't wait to see the look in your eyes as she sways over to you to feature her proud achievement. She has seen adults do this before. She has dreamed of the day that she finally could.

She worked at it. She took a risk. She is ready and comes over to you and says, "Look, I put my own shoes on, all by myself!" I hope you don't respond with, "They're on the wrong feet!" Recognize her progress and improvement. "Honey, you put your own shoes on, all by yourself. You must be proud of yourself. You are growing up, aren't you?"

4 **Communicate your confidence.** Goethe, the poet, conclude that, "If you want someone to develop a trait, treat them as though they already have it." Make a winner out of people. Communicate that you believe in them. They can do it!

Researchers have shown that when teachers have greater positive expectations for students, they actually help to provide a climate where students produce better grades. When bogus psychological reports were given to teachers, telling them that the I.Q. scores of individual were higher than they actually were, the teachers' elevated expectations of the students' abilities led to greater student achievement. In **Unconscious Conspiracy: Why Leaders Can't Lead**, Warren Bennis states, "In a study of school teachers, it turned out that when they had high expectations of their students, that alone was enough to cause an increase of up to twenty five points in the student's I.Q. scores.

Robert Schuller, founder of the concept of possibility thinking, reported on an elderly school teacher from New

York who had a high rate of success with students whose peers had a higher frequency of brushes with the law. When asked for the secret of her success, the teacher said, "I just loved those kids and believed in them."

If someone believes in us, and communicates that belief in us along with understanding and a feeling that what I do is important, I will have a tendency to take a second look at myself. Deep down I want that person to be right, so I may try to make it happen. The fact that some psychologists tell us that we use only 2–15% of our potential demonstrates that there is always room for improvement—in the context of an encouraging person.

What we expect is, more often than not, what we get.

5 **Choose understanding before judging:** Consciously choose to listen to understand another person based upon their vantage point. What does it look like from their world? Not how should it look to the other person according to my world.

A little lad comes home from school and says, "mommy, that mean teacher yelled at me in front of all the other kids." The average parent responds in judgment, "What did you do?"

The child of course, answers, "Nothing!" and shuts down

The listening parent imagines what it looks like and feels like from the child's perspective.

"Dillon, that must have been embarrassing, I mean being yelled at in front of your friends."

Dillion now opens up, tears in his eyes, "It was, mama."

And mom responds, "Would you like to tell me more about what happened today?"

"Ok mom."

Notice that, "Would you like to tell me more about what happened today? Is the same question as, "What did you do?" except that it works better. Listening to understand is a sure sign of practical intelligence.

6 **Help each person see how he or she fits in:** Alfred Adler argued that humans are socially rooted beings, and it is important for a person to see where he or she fits in.

"We really missed you while you were on vacation. We had less fun when our stand up comedian was away," helps a person see how they fit in, how they belong.

"Without you in the lineup, Bill, we have no power."

"As receptionist, you're the first lady of our business."

"You are a symbol to our team of the importance of teamwork, Ally."

Think of people you want to encourage and find ways of helping them to see how they fit in, what role they play, and how they belong. Their eyes will light up when you do.

7 **Point out each person's contribution to the world:** A day that will stand out in the history books for centuries to come is July 20, 1969. It was a day when humankind's grasp became closer to its reach. It was a day when the citizens of the planet Earth placed the first person on the moon, one quarter million miles away. It was a proud day for all Earthlings, especially Americans.

July 20, 1969 was an especially proud day for me. It was all because of a special meaning giving leader for who I worked. Let me explain the power of a meaning giving leader.

In the summer months from 1963-1967, I was employed by Carpenter Technology, a Reading, Pennsylvania based specialty steel company. My job was as a bundler. We bundled bars of steel over and over again for eight hours a day, six days a week. Sound boring? It could have been, but I was fortunate enough to have a far-sighted foreman who helped point out to each of us bundlers what we were really doing for the world.

"Part of what you guys are bundling today will be headed for Detroit and will become part of automobiles," the burly enthusiast might say at the beginning of the shift. But the one meaning giving day that I remember the most was when Mr. U confided, "This week most of what you fellas will be wrapping up to ship out is a specialty product designed to be a part of the first space vehicle like the one our government will eventually be landing on the moon."

Man did we bundle that day.

On that July day when American astronaut Neil Armstrong took his first step on the moon and voiced those words, "One small step for a man, one giant leap for mankind," I was nose up to the TV, tears in my eyes, waiting for him to give.... the list of credits!

I dreamed, "And to you, Lew Losoncy, for bundling those bars of Steel at Car Tech, we are here because of your efforts!"

I then thought about all of the other workers who didn't feel what I felt that day because they didn't have a meaning giving supervisor like Mr. U.

8 Use humor to help people accept what they won't change: Remembering our chapter on Acceptance and reality help people to humorously accept that, "What is, is!" I tell groups, "If its 90 degrees

and it is snowing outside, should it be snowing? Of course. Why? Because it is! What is, is!"

9 **Build excitement for change by associating change with growth:** There has never been a time where so much change is taking place in so many peoples' lives than today. And it will be even more tomorrow. In an earlier chapter we talked about the importance of becoming intrinsically motivated, building a cheerleader inside us, because the outside world is always in transition. We can't count on constancy in the outside world. So we need to build the security inside of ourselves.

People with practical intelligence, with inner security, realize that not only do they have to adapt quickly to change, but they need to find ways of welcoming and embracing a new ways of change. Finding refreshment and personal growth in change.

Have you experienced the look on peoples' face who resist change? Arms folded, head down, people who haven't developed their practical intelligence turn their frustration into anger, and even sometimes paranoia. Can you recall times going to a picnic when he watched the 80 year-old woman dancing to Britney Spears music outside in the hot pavilion, while some others wave their hands in disgust saying, "Look at her, with that crazy music?" She welcomed change. And was rewarded for it.

Wouldn't you like to be like her when you are 80? Are you listening to the music of today and trying to understand it? Or, do you remind yourself of your own mother and father's response to your music as a teen?

What changes do you face today? How can you develop your practical intelligence and find a way to make it refreshing?

Who do you know needs some of your encouragement to get a new view of things to help them through some tough changing times.

Bob Dylan was right when he said that the times they are a changing. The times are always a changing.

10 **Give credit rather than take credit:** president Ronald Reagan had a sign on his desk which read, "Nothing is impossible for the person who doesn't mind if someone else gets the credit."

So true. Make it a practice to be a credit giver, rather than a credit hog. If you have an idea, and someone else suggests it, resist the tendency to say, "I've been thinking of that for a long while," and instead respond, "What a great idea. How do you see us getting that started?"

My friend, Gust Zogas, was a master of giving credit. Gust is the longest lasting President of Pennsylvania Community Colleges. He pulled off the impossible expansion of an institution once rejected by taxpayers, now a place that has touched every single family in Reading, Pennsylvania. Gust works with people to get things down by involving their ideas, getting them to buy in and commit, and then spending most of the time giving the credit to those people. Everyone knows Gust will give you a fair shake. After decades of leadership and the right to have buildings named after him, Gust simply tells you that he didn't do anything. It was the great citizens of Berks County who built this phenomenon called RACC.

Some say be like Mike. I say, "Be like Gust!" Give credit, and let your credit come back to you in the form of inner satisfaction and outer achievement.

11 Use enthusiastic, upbeat words: The words we use are crucial in encouragement. Use words that create a winning, on the move, active, find-a-way feeling. Our words can be the propellants that stimulate the minds and hearts of people up over the hills and obstacles along the way. After reading the following group of words record your feelings:

closed

stale

dead

stagnant

same

common

lifeless

rut

boring

decayed

routine

ho-hum

Your feelings: _____

_____

_____

_____

_____

_____

_____

_____

Now record your feelings after reading these words:

crisp

on-the-move

uplifting

high

fresh

youthful

birth

bigger

original

new

ascend

virile

debut

prime

Your reactions to these words: _____

_____

_____

_____

_____

_____

There is a huge difference between telling a group, "Things look bad," than taking the same situation and saying, "We face an exciting challenge ahead of us. we are about to see our best days."

ENCOURAGING PEOPLE TO THINK ABOUT THESE QUESTIONS OR
(There must be 50 ways to find more meaning at work)

Personal Meaning

1. **Personal Growth:** How have I grown since I started with our company?

2. **Pride:** What accomplishments do I feel most proud in doing what I do?

3. **Self-esteem:** How has my work changed my belief in myself through the years?

4. **Creativity:** Where have I put my own ideas into my work that was meaningful?

5. **Security:** What security have I earned through the years on the job?

6. **Love:** What do I love most about my job?

7. **Courage:** What was my most courageous moment on the job?

8. **Challenge:** What is my biggest challenge today? How can I turn it into a positive?

9. **Vision:** What personal quality will I develop this year?

10. **Curiosity:** How can I use my curiosity to grow even further on the job?

Task Meaning

11. **Skill Refinement:** What skills have I developed since being here at the company?

12. **Task Mastery over Specific Tasks:** What have I learned to master, to do really well? Maybe I'm one of the best there is.

13. **Task Progress:** What area of my work am I most progressing at, perhaps because I've been opened to learn?

14. **Correction:** When was a significant moment when I learned a better way to do what I was doing, and I improved myself?

15. **Problem Solving:** What problem did our company have that I helped to solve?

16. **Future Improvement:** What task do I need to work on to make my future even better?

Career/Professional Meaning

17. **Professional Growth:** How have I grown, not personally, but professionally since being with our company?

18. **Previous Job Mastery:** What previous jobs have I had to learn and master?

19. **Recognition:** What recognition have I received from my work?

20. **Advancement:** What advancements have I made since I started with our company?

21. **Future Career Advancements:** What am I willing to work towards to make my future even better than today?

Social Meaning

22. **Rewarding relationships:** What rewarding relationships have I found here at our company?

23. **Attention:** Who notices me? Who offers support when I need it?

24. **Belonging:** With which group do I feel I belong?

25. **Contributing:** Who have I contributed to help become better?

26. **Encouraging:** Who do I believe in, or have supported?

Team Meaning

27. **Mutual Respect:** Who on the team do I respect, who, in return respects me?

28. **Mutual Progress:** With whom are we growing together?

29. **Synergy of Ideas:** With whom on the team do we brainstorm new ideas together and things just flow?

30. **Team Theming:** What makes our team special? How are we unique?

31. **Winning Team:** What have we accomplished together?

32. **Open Communications:** With whom can I communicate both the good news and the bad news about our work? Who can I be extremely honest with in offering better ways to improve our work?

33. **Contributing at a Team Level:** How have I made our team a better place?

Organizational Meaning

34. **Fulfilling Vision:** How am I helping fulfill our company's vision?

35. **Living Cultural Values:** Where was an example of when I truly lived out our company's values?

36. **Feeling Empowered:** In what areas do I feel our company trusts me to trust my self?

37. **Being the Difference:** How have I made a difference for our company?

38. **Future Contribution:** What could I give that I know the company needs to make it a better place?

Customer Meaning

39. **Customer Sensitivity:** As I walk a mile in our customer's shoes, what am I most aware of?

40. **Striving to Perfection in Services:** What are some examples where I fought for our customer?

41. **Customer Humanizing:** When have I consciously treated a customer as a unique, special, distinct, important human being, rather than just a number? What were the results?

Community Meaning

42. **Community Development:** how have I, through my work, made my community a better place?

43. **Professional Community:** In what ways have I advanced my profession in our community's eyes?

World Meaning

44. **Building a Better World:** What is the single thing that sticks out in my mind as to how I am building a better world?

45. **Touching Lives:** How many lives have I touched, directly or indirectly, through my work since being with our company?

Inspirational Meaning

46. **Self-actualizing at Work:** Where in my work am I moving toward becoming the person I am capable of becoming?

47. **Flow:** When am I most myself in my job, or when am I truly in a state of flow, lost in my work?

48. **Spirit:** What gives me the most satisfaction about my work? What brings my spirit to life?

49. **Passion:** What do I believe in, more than anything else, about my work?

50. **God at Work:** How am I inspiring a better universe and connecting to God, or my equivalent to the ultimate through my work?

Encouraging works better than blaming because encouragement communicates belief and hope. Consider those people closest to you and develop a plan to lift them up and bring them in. When you encourage someone you change their world. And yours.

Now, let's explore ways of developing your practical intelligence by keeping your own self going and growing, buoyed up by an optimistic approach to life.

7

OPTIMISM

Lifts Us More Than Blaming Our Challenges

Every human achievement started in the mind and heart of a spirited individual who believed that the dream could be realized. Humanity has progressed from living in caves, to climbing snow-packed mountains that soar almost five miles into the heavens, to living in vehicles that travel around the earth in a hour, to placing a flag on the moon. Optimists have cured diseases that have plagued the human body, but not the human spirit for centuries. All of these achievements, and more have been accomplished because of a few believers with an eye on the heavens, and a desire for improvement. They had a huge advantage. They were optimists.

Every success story has one thing in common. They operate out of deep conviction that every problem has a solution. In fact, every problem has as many solutions as there are optimistic people who are willing to put their chins up and seek success. Bertrand Russell enlightened us with his conclusion that, "In the vast realm of the alive, creative, human mind there were no limitations."

OPTIMISTS LOOK AT WHAT THEY CAN DO, AND DO IT: PESSIMISTS LOOK AT WHAT THEY CAN'T OR WON'T DO, AND GET FRUSTRATED

After graduating from college, I worked as a fifth grade teacher for a year. All enthused to teach, it wasn't look that my fires were dampened for teaching one lunch time. In the faculty room I was listening to some teachers talking about the futility of education.

"These kids now a days don't care. They're not like we were in my day. They just don't want to learn."

Another added, "And the parents today don't give you as a teacher the support today either. In my day if I went home and told my parents the teacher yelled at me, I'd get a good spanking."

It went on, "The school district doesn't respect its teachers today, either. The school board doesn't want to pay us what we are worth. They treat us like trash. Teaching is not like it used to be."

Listening to the litany of blames, I allowed myself to be sucked into the pain of professional uselessness. I left lunch and walked down the hallway thinking about quitting teaching at the end of the year and maybe becoming a weatherman or something. By the way I was walking, it must have looked like I was living between happy hours. And I felt a tap on my shoulder. I looked back and there was one of the happiest teachers in the school.

"What's the matter? Looks like you lost your best friend."

"What's the point of teaching," echoing the sentiment in the faculty room.

"The kids today don't care, the parents are against you, and the school district doesn't support you, and the school board doesn't want to pay us what we are worth."

The wise teacher smiled, took his folded newspaper from under his arm and pointed it to me as if to instruct. With the school bell ringing in the background, he asked me, "Where you just in the faculty room?"

I responded, "Yes, how do you know?"

You answered, "You sound just like them. Kid, you don't have to change these kid's pasts. You don't have to influence their parents. You don't have to be concerned about the school district, the school board, or for that matter the President of the United states. All you have to do is to have a great day with those 25 children who are with you this year. You have a year with 25 little human beings you can help believe in themselves this year. That's all. You are making your life too tough."

He smiled, walked down the hallway, and I heard him say to his class, "In the next 45 minutes, you are going to learn how airplanes fly, and you will remember it for the rest of your life. Are you ready?"

"Yeah!"

This teacher's view of life worked better than the faculty room pessimists. His view changed my life because he helped me to focus on what I can do, not what I can't or won't do.

IMPROVE YOUR VISION

Its all in the way you look at things. If your power system, your zest for life, is turned off, you can easily ignite the engines again by changing your attitude. Become your own optometrist today and make a decision to clear up your vision. Put on an enthusiastic set of eyeglasses in order to view yourself, other people and the world in a new way.

The philosopher William James, proclaimed that the greatest revolution of the century was the discovery that human beings, by changing the inner view of themselves in their minds, could change their outer world. Think of it. By changing the way you look at things, through your new set of eyeglasses towards life, you can actually change your life. The incredible story of William James, surely one of the most popular philosophers of all times, is a perfect example of the power of a person's view of life.

James suffered from severe depression and was even suicidal at times. James, like many people today, pondered the uselessness of his life, often seeing no reason to go on. He was pessimistic, believing that nothing really seemed to matter. James concluded that it was useless to work harder at life if nothing really mattered anyway.

In a letter to a friend, James expressed his hopelessness, "what's the use?" view of things. He described his fatalistic outlook on life and his belief that everything was predetermined. The return letter from his friend literally changed the academic world for decades just by changing James' view of his life. In this life changing letter, his friend urged him to wake up in the morning, set a goal, make a commitment to the goal and by day's end to see if that worked better than a pessimistic approach of nothing you can't affect your life.

James took his friends advice. The next day James started his winning streak on a optimistic not by changing his view of his day. Instead of believing that he was powerless and that nothing mattered, he concluded it was up to him to create his own optimism. This new view gave him the enthusiasm and energy necessary to meet the challenges of the day. With his new life outlook, or inlook his life changed dramatically. William James then began making monumental contributions to the disciplines of psychology and philosophy. In fact, James went on to help develop one of the major schools of philosophy called pragmatism.

Not coincidentally, pragmatism is the idea that truth is simply the process of finding beliefs that work. His previous hopeless, and negative ideas about life didn't work. Remember the pessimistic teachers in the faculty room whose negative ideas about life were causing themselves misery? Their ideas, no matter how accurate they were or weren't, didn't work to give them meaning and motivation, enthusiasm and energy.

When William James made a commitment each day to approach the day with optimism towards his life and his work, the new belief worked and he became productive. James became his own optometrist, changed his set of eyeglasses towards life and his life changed.

What does this mean to you? You give yourself a huge advantage when you wake up and make a commitment to proceeding optimistically towards the day.

CULTIVATE A PHILOSOPHY OF LIFE THAT WORKS

The poet Samuel Johnson wrote, "When there is no hope, there can be no endeavor." Hopelessness and pessimism create a fast downhill freefall. Hope and optimism are the fuels to power you past any cloudy weather. When looking up, look beyond the clouds and you will seeing the shining sun.

The sun is always there, but during a rainstorm in life, only the optimists see it.

Optimism is a better predictor of a person's positive motivation than is intelligence. In fact, sometimes intelligence and over analyzing gets in the way of getting things done. I recall being invited to participate in a noontime debate on a TV program. It was entitled, *"Life in the Late 70's: The Best or Worst Time to Live?"* I was going to debate someone whom I believe was one of the most brilliant people I had ever met.

Prior to the ten minute debate, I had the opportunity to spend a bit of time in the studio waiting room with my debate opponent, an advocate of fatalistic foundations. Even in the waiting room, his face wore a bitter, hopeless expression. To break the ice, I asked my opponent how long he thought he could talk about how horrible life was in the 70's. He responded that he could probably go on forever about how bad things were. He talked about injustices, economic atrocities, political pilfering, natural disasters, educational inefficiencies and moral decay. The genius of gloom went on to say that he had accumulated enough data to suggest that this was the worst time ever in the history of humankind to live.

At this point, a few minutes away from the actual debate, I glanced at my opponent's reams of discouraging data. Not having a single jotting to support my positive position, I felt a surge of unpreparedness. Because it was obvious that he had more information to present than I did, I offered my friend the opportunity to take some of my 5 minutes, along with his 5 to present his position. Without hesitation, he agreed to take not only his debate time, but four and one half minutes of my time. I would take the last 30 seconds.

A few minutes later, it was time for the debate to begin. The host explained the unusual procedure the debate was to follow and then introduced the purveyor of the pessimistic perspective. The professor's presentation commenced, and in only a few seconds it was obvious about how well versed he was on the topic. It seemed like he had spent a lifetime accumulating data to support the bleak view of life. His data was impeccable, his content was well organized, and his delivery was congruent with the facts. His topic on how life was channeled onto a catastrophic course was so effective, I have to admit that at moments in his monologue I felt sympathetic misery, sometimes angry, despair and hopeless. His presentation only missed having background music like "Eve of destruction," playing.

My time finally arrived. I took part of the 30 seconds commending him for his eye-opening presentation. I then turned to the professor who bronzed the gold medal of life the question, "Sir, does the view that you choose to give to your life work best? Does it make you happy and productive.?

Does your view of life work for you? If it doesn't, sounds like there's no downside risk in developing a new view. To be successful, it is important to realize that our view is more important than the facts. And the significant realization is not how intelligent you are, but rather how you can use your IQ to make things better. Using your intelligence as the professor did, to gather data about how bad things are, is unproductive busy work that certainly cannot make one happy. All of the negative data about life that can be amassed is sterile in the mind of a positive enthusiast who believes things can get better and quickly moves to make things happen. The professor's ideas were accurate, but they didn't work. Create an outlook on life that works and make a difference by proceeding optimistically. And when we proceed optimistically, we are going forward lifted up with the conviction that our problems have solutions.

Always interested in the history of humankind knows that there were always problems to challenge the human mind and heart. And that there were always people, most, in fact, who responded to these problems by griping, whining, blaming, complaining and giving up. And then there were the others who saw the same problems, and fired up their optimistic determination and looked for solutions. And it is a simple fact that the whole human lot has progressed because of these rare, but treasured optimists, who, despite the odds, rejected the useless course of worrying, or wallowing in the dreaded course of pessimism. That's why you don't have any streets in your hometown named after pessimists. And you probably have never been to a testimonial dinner for a nit picker.

PUT YOUR POSITIVE VIEW INTO ACTION

An optimist, even under the most difficult outside challenges knows that the only challenge is life is within oneself. The challenge to go on and on. Such a positive doer was Terry Fox. The young, handsome Canadian lad, at the height of his athletic career was told that he had cancer in his right leg. The disease was rapidly spreading towards other parts of his body, forcing the need to amputate his leg. The sudden news shattered Terry's original lifetime dreams.

Terry Fox had to make a choice. Blame the world or make something happen? Which course do you think is more likely to work?

Instead of running away, the optimistic lad began the "Marathon of Hope," to help raise funds for cancer research. He took on the challenge of literally running, with the assistance of an artificial leg, from Eastern to Western Canada, a distance of over 3,000 miles. Unfortunately Terry didn't succeed in reaching Vancouver because the cancer in his leg spread to his lungs and eventually to the rest of his body.. After running halfway across the continent, he was hospitalized and shortly afterward, he died.

But Terry Fox did succeed in other ways. He not only raise millions of dollars for cancer research, he inspired all Canadians, and others throughout the world with the truth that we can overcome our challenges, by first believing, and second by showing up and doing. He made us all realize that we all can count. Terry brought people together to work toward common goals, and he brought the goodness out in all of us.

"Somewhere the hurting must stop," Terry hoped. Cancer will be beaten someday because of people like Terry.

You might say that the optimist, who takes action, always has a leg to stand on.

OPTIMISTS WHO TAKE ACTION LIVE ON

One optimist who got things done was Irwin Westheimer. The year was 19093. While at work one morning, the twenty-three year old man glanced through his office window and observed a young boy searching through a garbage can for food. Irwin Westheimer was touched, but more practically, he was determined to take action. The pessimist might dissertate or decry the social injustices or even envision the doom of humankind over an additional glass of wine. Not Irwin. He went out to bring the boy into his office. Irwin fed the boy, went to his home to meet his mother, and eventually found employment for her. But the young optimist didn't stop there. Irwin went to the members of his club and encouraged each of them to do the same with other impoverished youth in their community.

At age 101 Irwin Westheimer died. Or did he? No, because he continues to live in the hearts of a half million boys who are still being touched by his optimistically-based actions. These fatherless boys feel a sense of importance each time they play catch with a "Big Brother." Irwin Westheimer was the founder of the Big Brothers of America. Surely thousands of people see or read about children eating out of garbage cans. But Irwin was a doer, who saw the problem, and moved towards a solution.

OPTIMISTS GO ON
EVEN AGAINST ALL ODDS

Another optimist who made a huge difference was Marva Collins. She is a Chicago school leader, an optimistic doer. Frustrated by the public schools, she formed her own school, the Westside Preparatory School. Soon after her school opened she had sixth graders reading at the college level. She threw away the "See Sun Run" books and introduced her elementary school children to Shakespeare, Plato, Aristotle, Emerson, and other classic writers. A powerful achievement, wouldn't you say?

Yes, but the achievement is even more powerful than that. You see, Westside accepts only those students who are either expelled or are failing miserably in the public schools. The student body at Westside is composed of children labeled either, "mentally retarded," "incorrigible," or suffering from some form of learning disability.

Initially, Marva Collins used her home on Chicago's tough westside as the classroom for her 18 pupils. In five years time, she had 200 pupils aged 4-14, and seven teachers housed in a school building with six classrooms. Westside currently has a waiting list of several thousand.

All of this, because of one person. Marva Collins saw a problem, took action and made a difference against all odds. Again, if she hadn't acted on hope, there would not have been any.

The world is a better place because of Terry Fox, Irwin Westheimer and Marva Collins. And hopefully, you.

DEVELOPING YOUR OPTIMISTIC EXPLANATORY STYLE

A form of practical intelligence is the ability to find the most workable view to handle setbacks. In his book, *Learned Optimism*, Philadelphia psychologist, Dr. Martin Seligman outlined a breakthrough concept on optimism. Seligman observed how optimists and pessimists explain setbacks to themselves in different ways. He called how we explain a setback, our, "explanatory style." Seligman's ideas are powerful and can change your life in one reading.

There are three major differences in how optimists and pessimists explain a setback to themselves. Pessimists tend to take the viewpoints that setbacks are personal, permanent and pervasive. That is, when something happens to a pessimist, such as a rejection, or not getting a job, the pessimist concludes, (1) "I'm no good, (personal), (2) "I'll never be any good," (permanent), and (3) "I'll never be able to do anything right, (pervasive).

Imagine how you would feel if every time you experienced a setback, you took these three viewpoints from your experience. Would you ever be motivated to try anything again? Not very much practical intelligence in a negative explanatory style because it doesn't work to advance someone.

The positive person, or optimist, tends to choose a different explanatory style to respond to the very same setback. The optimist, after reflection, takes these three vantage points: (1) "The situation wasn't right," (situation related, rather than personal, (2) "I'll get the next job," (temporary, rather than permanent), (3) "It won't affect any other area of my life," (situation related rather than pervasive).

Imagine the lifting advantage that having an optimistic explanatory style can offer. By viewing a setback, as an optimist does, we urge ourselves to go forward, rather than catastrophize and give up. Please read Seligman's many books and you will be developing your practical intelligence.

Your beliefs shape your destiny. The optimist, who holds go forward beliefs, goes forward. There is no downside risk to being an optimist!

USE THE BEST AS MODELS FOR YOUR LIFE

Abraham Maslow transformed the thoughts of the community of psychologists when he outright challenged the ideas of Sigmund Freud on the possibilities of people. Freud, who worked with very seriously disturbed humans a hundred years ago, was pessimistic about the human's ability to rise above their limited biology. Maslow decided to find other models to draw from, and he studied the healthiest, most fulfilled humans whom he called, "self-actualized." Like a seed becoming a giant oak, when in an actualizing state, humans are able to fully express themselves. They use more of their potential. You could say that they have really developed their practical intelligence because their use of their fuller potential works a lot better than operating out of our lower view of self.

In ***The Farther Reaches of Human Nature***, Maslow wrote:

> "*If you want to answer the question as to how tall the human species can grow, then obviously it is wise to pick out the ones who are already the tallest and study them. If we want to know how fast a human can run, then it is of no use to average out the speed of a sample of the population; it is far better to collect Olympic gold medal winners and see how well they can do. If we want to know the possibilities for spiritual growth, value growth or moral development in human beings, then I maintain that we can learn the most by studying our most moral, ethical and saintly people.*"

> "*I think that it is fair to say that human history is a record of the ways in which human nature has been sold short. The highest possibilities of human nature have practically always been underrated. Even when good specimens, the saints, the sages, the great leaders of history, have been available for study, the temptation has been too often to consider them not human, but supernaturally endowed.*"

Build your practical intelligence. Identify with the best, not the average. Surround yourself with people who have the qualities you want to develop.

OPTIMISTS MOVE TO POSITIVE CLIMATES

The best way to learn French is to live in France for a few years, and to associate with French speaking people. Associate with people who have the qualities you want to acquire. Never get advice from someone who hasn't achieved what you'd like to achieve. Don't go up to a down and out person who is constantly blaming the world and ask for advice. Don't ask someone who hates their work, "What's your secret?" They don't know.

If you want to be a millionaire, and you wonder if it is possible, don't ask someone who is bankrupt. They will tell you, "no!" But what happens if you ask the same question to a millionaire. They will respond, "Yes, of course!"

Be careful where you get your advice. Move yourself in circles that have positive climates.

APPOINT A HONORARY BOARD
OF POSITIVE ADVISORS FOR YOURSELF

Remember that you are the CEO of your life. You are also the Director of Environmental Engineering. Hire uplifting people who have developed their practical intelligence. People whose philosophy of life that works. Here is my board of people I turn to imagining what they would do if faced with situations I am facing. They may be living or not.

And in many instances I haven't even met them. But I sure get a lift when I bring them mentally into my office and ask each one individually, what is your advice for me?

Dr. Jonas Salk, found cure for polio

Arnie & Sydell Miller, founders of Matrix Essentials

Michael Jordan, athlete

Al Neuharth, founder USA Today Newspaper

Dr. Richard Cahn, friend and upbeat professor at Kutztown university

John Kennedy, former President

Lance Armstrong, motivator

Elizabeth Marshall, aunt, stand up comedienne

Make up your own list of Optimistic Board members:

BOARD OF POSITIVE ADVISORS

1. _____

2. _____

3. _____

4. _____

5. _____

IF YOU CAN'T DO EVERYTHING, DO SOMETHING

What would you like to achieve during your lifetime? What challenges in the world would you like to make a commitment to overcome? How would you like to make the world a better place?

What is your plan? What first step would you like to take? When will you take it?

FIND A WAY TO YOUR DREAMS JUST BECAUSE SOMETHING IS IMPOSSIBLE DOESN'T MEAN IT CAN'T BE DONE

At times the word "impossible," has a way of intimidating even the best in us. I guess its because impossible sounds like an absolute, unbending and immovable. In actuality, impossible is a relative term.

The impossible is relative to time and to technology. A hundred years ago, if someone had said a spacecraft would fly a quarter million miles to the moon and a person would walk out and place a flag into the moon's surface, everyone would have felt that was impossible.

Yes, the impossible is relative to time and to technology. But mainly, the impossible is relative to the individual's creative determination and Find-a-Way Spirit! The possible is not defined by what lies outside of us, but by what lies inside us. The major choice people make for their life is to whether they want to spend their life energies finding things to blame for why they can't get ahead, or using their time to challenge themselves onward to greater achievements.

When you are dreaming of the possible inside yourself, confront the part of you that is looking to blame, look up to the star light sky, and in the center you'll see the illuminated moon. Then remind yourself that there is a flag on the moon. The challenge ahead of you may be impossible. But just because its impossible, doesn't mean it can't be done. It means the world needs you to do it.

Develop your practical intelligence by choosing a view of life that will work to keep you going. Optimism is a big part of that commitment.

You have a choice; you can blame, or you can claim your fame!

REFERENCES

Csikszentmihalyi, Mihaly. Flow: *The Psychology of Optimal Experience*. New York: Harper & Row, 1990.

Ellis, Albert and Robert Harper. **A New Guide to Rational Living.** Hollywood, California: Wilshire Books, 1975.

Kohn, Alfie. *The Brighter side of Human Nature*. New York: Basic Books, 1990.

Losoncy, Lewis. *Turning People On: How to Be an Encouraging Person.* Sanford, Florida. InSync Communications, 2000.

Losoncy, Lewis and Diane Losoncy. *What is, is: How to Accept What You Can't Change & Change What You Can*. Boca Raton, Florida: St. Lucie Press, 1997.

Maslow, Abraham. *The Farther Reaches of Human Nature.* New York: Viking Press, 1971.

Rogers, Carl. *On Becoming a Person.* Boston: Houghton-Mifflin,1961.

About the Diogenes Consortium

**If you found this book thought provoking...
If you are interested in having this author...
or other of our consulting authors
design a workshop or seminar for your
company, organization, school, or team...**

Let the experienced and knowledge group of experts at
The Diogenes Consortium go to work for you. With literally hundreds of years of combined experience in:

*Human Resources • Employee Retention
Management • Pro-Active Leadership • Teams
Encouragement • Empowerment • Motivation
Energizing • Delegating Responsibility
Spirituality in the Workplace
Presentations to start-ups and Fortune 100 companies,
tax-exempt organizations and schools
(public & private, elementary through university)
religious groups and organizations*

**Call today for a list of our
authors/speakers/presenters/consultants**

Call toll free at:
866-602-1476

Or write to us at:
2445 River Tree Circle
Sanford, FL 32771